Colours of the Goldfields

Goldfields Writers Group

A catalogue record for this book is available from the National Library of Australia

ISBN: 1 876922 30 3
ISBN-13: 978-1-876922-30-6

Linellen Press
265 Boomerang Road
Oldbury, Western Australia
www.linellenpress.com.au

Foreword

The idea for this book was suggested by Bettina, a reporter from the Kalgoorlie Miner at that time. Bettina started the group in 2012, but has since moved away from the Goldfields with her family. Before she left, however, she arranged with the Boulder Rotary to donate to the Goldfields Writers Group a book grant of $2,000. The money was raised by the Rotary's Annual radio auction. Thank you to Bettina and Boulder Rotary. Any other funding has come from the members of the group.

We have had many different writers attending the meetings at the library over the years. Kalgoorlie and the Goldfields in general, has a shifting population, unfortunately writers came and went …

I have been involved with Goldfields Writers almost from its inception. In the last few years we have had a steady band of writers, most of whom are also artists, but not all. We have a Minister of the Church and several school teachers, young people, mums and dads. Unfortunately, the male attendance is a little slim these days.

We aim to have several workshops every year, often during the Artgold, Heart of Gold Festival. We have been lucky to have the benefit of visits every one or two years from The Society of Women Writers WA, who hold workshops for everyone (all Goldfielders and some of their own members) in the Railway Hotel.

Lesley Nazzari

Artist contributors

Horse drawings – Leila Worth
Russian Choir – Gudrun Sahm
Emu, Butcher Bird and Kangaroo –Sheryl Fasolo
Zentangle Bird – Lesley Nazzari
Phone sketches: Giraffe Kiss, Lost child found – Lesley Nazzari
Brian Nazzari portrait, Magpie, Crow, Cat, Many Faces – Ryan Nazzari
Eugene Winter portrait – Eugene Winter

Photos by Donnie Martin:

- Lake Perkolilli
- Church in Egan Street, Kalgoorlie
- Gum leaves in Kalgoorlie
- Bush near Coolgardie
- Grass tree near Mt Burges
- Sand plain near Mt Burges
- Field naturalists exploring Caenyie rock
- Exchange Hotel, corner Maritana and Hannan Sts, Kalgoorlie.

Photos by Lesley Nazzari:

- The Bridge, Karlkurla Park, Kalgoorlie
- Lake Ballard, outside Menzies, north of Kalgoorlie
- Paddy Hannan statue after a sudden storm
- Peace Park
- Brindi
- Bella

Photo by Ruth Koedyk

- Clouds

Unknown Photographer:

- Two old prospectors, Len and Bluey
- Partly reconstructed Coolgardie Wagon
- Bluff, Coolgardie

Contents

Acknowledgments

Thanks to everyone who has helped or been involved with the development of our group:

Bettina, Elizabeth S, The Society of Women Writers WA and Anne Pettit, who has also held regular workshops in Kalgoorlie (the latter group and Anne are based in Perth).

Thank you to Sheryl Fasolo and her husband, Silvano, for all the work towards the book.

Thank you to the members who have helped by holding workshops, to the editors and proof readers – Glenda, Sheryl, Donnie and Ruth – and to our members for their interest and written contributions.

Thank you to Janet Bartle for allowing us to use her artwork for the cover and the artists who contributed drawings and/or photos.

Thank you, writers, for turning up once (or twice) a month.

Thank you to Helen Iles for her efforts in finally making the book happen.

Thank you to the City of Kalgoorlie Boulder for the use of the Library and the very helpful library staff at the William Grundt Memorial Library, Robert Street, Kalgoorlie.

Thank you to anyone else who has helped in any way.

Goldfields Writers Group acknowledges the Traditional Owners and pays respect to their physical, spiritual and cultural connection to the country.

We are all visitors to this time, this place. We are just passing through. Our purpose is to observe, to learn, to grow, to love … and then we return home.

Australian Aboriginal proverb

Preface

The Goldfields Writers Group was formed in 2012 and meets at the public library in Kalgoorlie Boulder every 2nd Thursday and 4th Sunday of the month at 2pm. We share passages we have written, respond to the challenges of different subjects and learn about other writers and their work.

Our members include generational Goldfielders, and settlers from other parts of Australia and from a number of different countries around the world.

This book of verse and prose presents the reader with a selection of diverse and interesting outlooks of life in the Goldfields of Western Australia, glimpses into our pasts and shared personal experiences.

The Goldfields Writers Group are pleased to present –

Colours of the Goldfields.

Sheryl Fasolo

Workshop for Artgold

Travis Carraro

Travis was raised in Newcastle, NSW, and came to Kalgoorlie in 2010 to work as a radiographer at the hospital. Though he prefers science fiction and crime, the Goldfields Writers Group did allow him to expand and see different things. He left in 2016, but the memory of the Goldfields and people within will always remain.

One Week in Kalgoorlie

I know no one
I have seen most
This place is old
This town is lost

The heat is difficult
The air is dust
The dirt is red
Plants barely break the crust

Rundown groups abound
Certain places elicit fear
I am pessimistic,
But there is community here.

One Year in Kalgoorlie
I know many
I have seen much…but not all
This place has history
The city says survival

The heat is tolerable
The air is dusty but clean
The ground is multi layered
Not every plant needs to be green.

Pipeline

It starts in the Perth hills,
From there, snaking outward, on.
Many towns supplied.

Cunderdin next stop
An open flat town resides
Dry; a long way to go.

Merredin appears,
Wheat is central to this place
Almost half way there

Same track, road, water
Yebillon near Bodallin
Greenery is sparse

Then woodland returns,
Ghooli contains the next leg,
Goldfields have begun.

Gilgai, Dedari,
Final flow stations before
Terminating, point.

Mount Charlotte lookout,
This place is not a mountain,
Small hill, Reservoir

Paddy Hannan statue Hannan Street, Kalgoorlie, after a sudden storm

Coral Carter

Coral Carter was born and educated in Kalgoorlie. As well as writing poetry she is the publisher of Mulla Mulla Press. She produced her first collection *Descended from Thieves* in 2012; in 2013 was a guest at the Queensland Poetry Festival and inaugural Writer-in-Residence for the Northern Territory Writers Centre. She reads most weeks at Perth Poetry Club.

One Morning When

One morning when
The clothesline was strung with water beads
The power line was hung with galahs
I saw…
A black shouldered hawk hunched
On a lookout post
A hoodie of clouds pulled over his head

Hunting birds grow thin in winter
As reptiles sleep the cold away
And small birds hide from rain

I saw…
A grey and white cat
Squashed on the highway
Between bush and streets
Its belly full of natives
Clawed from lower branches
Its greedy guts mashed into well-kept fur
A grind of mince under CAUTION WIDE LOAD wheels
The head still intact
Popped eyes stared in the direction of a fireside

Partly reconstructed Wagon, Coolgardie

Sheryl Fasolo

I was born in New Zealand but for the last 40 years have resided in the Goldfields of WA, raising our family here also. I enjoy portraying the 'colours' of the bush by both pen and brush. I take pleasure in sharing some of that enjoyment.

Fog in May

I stride along the path
In the freshness of the dawn
Clouds dance across the dumps
Trailing ribbons, pink and torn
The sun prepares to rise.

A colder, ruffling wind
Combs through the trees
Grey, jagged sheets of cloud
Drift with the southern breeze
The blinding orb is veiled.

Galahs huddle on the lines
Ghosted gums stand all around
Orbs of yellow dragons' eyes
Pierce the shroud with muted sound
In solid form, race by.

High above in realms of light
Sitting huddled, circling round
Frustrated, anxious eyes survey
The blanket on the ground.
The plane returns to Perth.

Cold, damp tentacles invade
My clothes, my hands, my face
Insidious fingers chill my spine
No sun, no day, this dreary place
Back to warmth and home.

The Unwary Campers

Along the dusty road
That leads from here to there
The tired travellers view
With heartfelt shed of tear
A perfect place to camp the night
And breathe the fresh bush air.

The jeep draws to a halt
Its people tumble out
They gaze in rapt approval
At the trees and bushes near
"We'll camp on soft dry sand
In that gully over there"

The tent gets hammered well
Right into the ground
The fire lit, dinner cooked
The campers gather round
While birds flit by atwitter
Amazed such fools abound

"Don't be such a Drongo,"
I can almost hear them say
"Don't go camping near the creek
'Cause just up north, ahead
A storm's been brewing,
Fair fit to raise the dead."

In hills far, far away
The storm has rained its rain
Water gathers, rivers run
Through every dip and plain
And it's coming, coming fast
As relentless as a train

Gazing up at stars so bright
Glad the storm's so far away
The campers settle for the night
To dream the hours away
In sweet anticipation
Of rest and fun next day

Alas round midnight hours
Comes a swishing sort of sound
A racing wall of water
Descending down the creek
Sweeping everything away
Swamps campers, tent and jeep

"Don't be such a Drongo,"
I can almost hear them say
"Don't go camping near the creek
'Cause just up north, ahead
A storm's been brewing
'Twill wash away your tent and bed."

Coolgardie to Kalgoorlie-Boulder

Passing through Coolgardie
– on our way to Kal-
A spacious little town
Wide, wide streets and buildings
Dotted round.

Comes terrain sparse, bared
Dissected by roads, trucks
Blasted ground by sun and man
Hills, valleys lost
And formed.

Passing dusty, lonely roads
Solitary, hidden in the bush
Prospectors ply their trade
The everlasting quest
For gold.

Then we see upon the left,
A vast clearing opening wide
Trampled by a thousand feet
Trees don't grow where the cameleers
Once camped

Eucalypts and bush line the way we go
Shiny trunks, glistening leaves,
Broom bush, wattle, saltbush,
Stands of Silver Gimlet, misty grey
With green

37 k is the sealed road we travel
Sometimes a mining road veers off
Sometimes to dam or station,
And tracks to nowhere
In particular

Or to Kurrawang
Once a little mission town
Still a pleasant place to live
With school and church
And grounds

Then from Seven Mile Hill
A vista lines the east
Extending to the north from south
Vast mining dumps, some tanks
Headframes

Down the hill a road veers off
To Lake Douglas, recreation,
Along the straight, one headframe beckons
The bush and woodlands still
Rush by.

Soon buildings intersperse with bush,
Industrial shops, big trucks.
They fade, suburbia begins
Kalgoorlie-Boulder
We've arrived!

Jeremiah G.

Jeremiah G. with the big brown eyes,
Clever hands and the jet black hair.
Bold you stand king of all you see
Your subjects serve on bended knee.

Jeremiah G. open wide your arms
You're as free as the roos, goannas, galahs
You're part of this land from way back in time
Its deserts and hills with salt lakes entwined.

Jeremiah G. with the soft brown skin
Untouched, as yet, by the harsh summer sun
Go to your mama, cuddle up tight
And listen to stories as the moon shines bright.

Summer Dreaming

When it's hot in Kal
And summer heat shimmers
Over sun baked land

I dream of the sparkling sea
Feeling the cool damp sand

When the Willy-Willy
Wanders stirring up dust
Making me sneeze

I dream of fish, gorgeous shells
A lovely fresh sea breeze

When the big trucks drone
Down the pit, up the dumps
In endless labour

I dream of squalling seagulls
Of boats in the harbour

When it's too hot to move
From air-conditioned rooms
In the house or store

I sigh and dream of walking
On the beautiful, cool sea shore

When it's hot in Kal

I dream of Esperance

Hurricane Hannah

On top of the table
Just a typical two
Stands the tiniest 'hurricane'
We ever knew.

Disaster is littered
All over the floor
From mother's bedroom
Down to the back door

Mum thought all was safe
With the doors fast shut
Till Hannah found chairs
She could push and climb up.

Who scattered the Lego?
It's a terrible mess!
John's not very happy
It's Hannah, we guess.

We all paint on paper
But quick as a hare
Hannah has painted
The wall, door and chair!

The schoolroom is quiet
We busily write
But Hannah is busy,
Finding something to bite.

Into the fridge
There's not a safe spot
Our Hannah can find it
Milk, chocolate, the lot

Hannah is clever
She's got it down pat
She can wash dishes
Flood bench, floor and mat!

We <u>do</u> love our Hannah
She's so cute! We adore
But we'll all hold our breath,
Till she's 'least three…or four!

Jacaranda Time

when gentle winds faze
through violet haze
and dance
in dappled light

when fingers soft brushed 
with royal blush
sway
'gainst mortared height

when naked limbs clothed
with chiffon mauve
dance
in dappled light

Silvano Fasolo

I have lived in the Goldfields of Western Australia since 1975 and with my wife, Sheryl, have raised our three daughters.

Being a teacher by profession, I have worked closely with a wide range of people. This includes folk of various nationalities, and more particularly, with local and desert Aboriginal people.

I have assisted in the development of a number of publications including Aboriginal language, tutorials and stories.

Bridge at Karlkula Park
Kalgoorlie-Boulder

Stew-it!

There was a young fellow named Stewart
Who cooked an old rabbit, to chew it
But to bring to the boil
Proved way too much toil
So said with a sigh, I'll just stew it!

Lake Ballard, near Menzies, north of Kalgoorlie

Sara Johnston

Happily married and mum to three young boys, I love to write. Whilst I relocated back to Queensland with my family a few years ago, the Goldfields and in particular Kalgoorlie will always hold a very dear place in my heart.

The Clearing

Wandering through the Goldfields bush
Without a destination in mind
Admiring the flora and fauna alike
Excited by what I may find.

Stepping over small bushes,
Navigating dry creek beds
When suddenly, a clearing
Filled with yellows, greens and reds.

The beauty of a clearing
With all its textures to explore;
Each clearing is so similar that
I may have stood here before.

An area for animals to gather,
Unhindered by shade they sunbake.
A clearing in the bush is indeed
A very special place.

Peace Park, Kalgoorlie

Jay Lassey

Jay attended the writing meetings a few times. She became interested in writing after doing a life story for the ABC. Jay is a friendly lady, who has raised a large family. She has many interests and consequently leads a busy life. Jay now lives in Perth, but returns to the Goldfields now and then.

My Pot of Gold

I drove from Melbourne to outback Queensland. While working in a pub, I rang home – my call was connected by an operator, who was having a good listen as I confessed to my Mum why I was running. The operator informed the owner of the hotel, and I was advised to go straight home, sort it out, get it right, but of course that's not what I did. Instead, I drove around the block and headed north. After driving through a heavy rain on a slimy dirt road, I'd wondered why cars and trucks were parked on the side of the road, while I skidded past.

Arriving at Charleville, everyone asked where I came from.

I replied, "Cunnamulla".

They all exclaimed, "No-one drives that 200 km road in the rain. It's far too dangerous!"

It's amazing what adrenaline will give you the power to do when you are scared!

I rang my mum on an STD phone and told her I was going to live in Darwin. North I headed. Picking up some hitch hikers, we conversed for 23 hours about children born blind, or incomplete, people starving, and many fascinating topics.

After arriving in Darwin, within three days I'd managed to find accommodation and two jobs. I was working as a receptionist in an uptown hairdressing salon Monday to Friday, then as a hairdresser on Saturday mornings. On weekends I worked the midnight shift at the International Bar in the Darwin Airport. I used drugs to keep me awake all weekend, returning to work on Mondays in a foul mood. Hence, that job only lasted a few months.

Meeting a guy with a Suzuki 110, the biggest motor bike in its time, we headed for Perth, along with what seemed like most of Darwin's population. We took three weeks to slowly make our way down the coast, stopping and enjoying different places, and meeting up with the same people repeatedly. This was the highlight of my life, the most amazing!

A year later I was forced to return to Melbourne to face what I was running from: the law. Miraculously I escaped incrimination, and returned to Perth. How could I have imagined the U turn my life was about to take! 180 degrees!

Attending a concert one evening, of gospel music and drama, a young guy spoke briefly, as though he was talking directly to me, telling me about my life.

That night I prayed a simple prayer; I received forgiveness and was "born again". No one could have told me how great that would be. Being forgiven! I could type pages trying to describe what happened that Saturday, May 31st, 1981, but you won't get it, unless you experience it for yourself. Like falling in love, losing my appetite, I was off my face! This beat any drug I'd ever tried! A light turned on, the sky became bluer, and trees really were greener.

Suddenly I had purpose. I knew I was here for a reason. Things made sense. I honestly couldn't have dreamed in my wildest imagination (and it is pretty wild) that I ever could have had such an experience! I found the pot of gold at the end of the rainbow. And the pot was full of gold for me to share with everyone I knew.

Thirty-three years later, it's fuller of gold than ever!

A Stash of Cash in the Trash

Mum was extremely clever with her money: she always kept a little bit aside. She secretly hid it away.

One time my parents were invaded by thieves at knife point. Dad insisted there was no money anywhere. They tied Mum to a chair, and threatened Dad. He promised them he had no more money than what he had given them. To Dad's astonishment, Mum disclosed the cash that was secretly stashed in the back room …

Now stripped of a further $3,000, Dad was stunned more than surprised, and scared that the thieves would believe he'd been lying.

It's a trait I inherited from my Mum. Raising six kids, there was never quite enough to have any left to spare. It didn't matter how little or how much we had, if I didn't start stashing now, I never would. The first ten percent always went to the Lord. (It's called a tithe). So we always had enough no matter how little we had. I figured a couple more dollars could be salvaged without us starving.

For years I did this, finally being able to purchase things we might never have saved for: a dual cab ute, which was a much deserved present for my hubby; a new leather lounge suite for the family to sit on.

Then, as time went by, it became obvious there was always a stash. I could hide it no longer and it began getting swallowed up by bills that needed to be paid. Consequently, it lost its thrill.

Some years later, while I was away in hospital one week, Hubby, not even considering the possibility of a stash, chose to bless me by cleaning out some drawers. How could he have known there was cash so craftily hidden amongst all the stuff in those drawers? I'd become very surreptitious over the years. A bunch of fifties was carefully concealed between some old advertising pamphlets.

And.... yes, he'd thrown them in the trash.

Thank God I'd needed to return to hospital that day, otherwise I wouldn't have needed to open that drawer. It was rubbish bin day. Any minute the bin would be emptied.

A mad dash to the green bin, feverishly depositing the contents on the ground. Diligently searching through each piece of trash, he found the stash of cash. Relieved beyond belief, and with a few stern looks, it was decided to use this second chance eight hundred dollars creatively. Instantly from my bed that day it became well received gifts for family and friends in need.

So why am I like Mum with cash? Is it because she took me away on the holidays we may never have afforded? Though as a child I'm sure it wouldn't have occurred to me what we could afford. Or was it the new ultra-modern furniture she kept producing. Could it truly be an Australian trait?

I'm not really sure. I am glad I have it though and if Mum were around I'd most definitely thank her.

Bush near Coolgardie

Ruth Koedyk

Immigrating to Australia from England in 1977, the Goldfields of WA has been my home for 40 years. I live in Kalgoorlie with my husband and two dogs, travelling regularly to Perth where our two daughters now live. Retired from teaching, I gained an Associate Degree in Visual Art in 2010 and am now a qualified Art Therapist.

I am a visual artist interested in using a wide variety of materials to create ideas often inspired by the natural world. Through the Goldfields Writers Group I have found the companionship and inspiration to develop my creative writing skills in an atmosphere of mutual encouragement. Creating through writing and visual art has a harmony which I find very fulfilling.

Clouds

To watch clouds moving
You must lie ever so still
The sky hangs over you
Like a painting

They float by
Icebergs floating in a bowl of blue
Seen from space

Lie still
Watch time go by
Just for a moment

Table Leg

We fought over a table leg
My one true love and I,
The cruel words spoken
Were enough to make me cry.

We took our time in separate space
To let our hurt hearts heal
Until we felt at one again
To sit and share a meal

We sat around the table
And shared our thoughts
The same
It was that blinking table
That really was to blame.

This was written from a story told to her by a friend.

Coming Home

The sweetness of the familiar
The feel of the past like a well-worn blanket
The same stars over the house
In the cold winter sky
The chill coming round the back
Like there'd only ever been today.
The clock chimes like the door bell, and every year
Stands still as a row of books.
Coming home is like there'd never been anything but now.

The Waiting Game

Sometimes there's nothing to do but wait.
Wait for the tide to turn, the wounds to heal,
The pain to pass, the grief to fade.

Wait for the morning,
Wait for the bus,
Sit still or pace a while,
Fume a bit, fuss.

Wait for your turn in the shuffling queue
You're waiting and waiting
What else can you do?

Try crying your heart out
Try shouting out loud
Try yelling at someone
You need to be heard.

Try taking deep breaths
While closing your eyes
Then visualise green fields and fishing and skies
Try thinking of all the things that you *hate*
And top of the list will be
I HATE TO WAIT!

George Long

George is an elderly gentleman, a widower and a father of two sons and a daughter. George became a member of the writing group almost from its inception. When he began writing with the group we had other male members, however, for some time George was the only male. He found being outnumbered by women a bit disconcerting.

George loved to read. He liked to write about his early family history and also the history of the Goldfields. His writing often showed his keen sense of humour.

George was unwell a while back. He is well now but no longer attends the meetings.

.

Earth Quake Kalgoorlie, 2010

My recollections of this event were as follows: I was jogging up Boulder Road approaching the YMCA corner when there was a loud bang.

My first impression was that it was something in the mine (Superpit). I stopped running and scanned the horizon for dust clouds. There were none showing. I then carried on to home (York St.) and had my routine early morning siesta.

When I came to and drove around an hour or so later I discovered that some of the town – the Burt Street area – was closed to traffic. The worst hit buildings seemed to be in the central Burt Street area and Lane Street. They soon became covered with scaffolding.

I read an article in the Kalgoorlie Miner some time later which pin-pointed the actual fault as the corner of Lane and King Street and approximately 1,500 metres deep.

Not being a building type person and having been retired for some time, I was not affected directly.

One of my friends who was a self-employed electrical installer was actually called in to do some repairs on one of the pubs, which is now back in use, with some plating in the upstairs brickwork.

The worst hit buildings seem to have been a two-storey boarding house on the corner of Burt Street, opposite Digger Daws Oval, and, of course, the Golden Eagle Hotel opposite Boulder Primary School. Both of these buildings have since been demolished.

There have been two stages of repairs since then, with the second and final being perhaps government money and that seems to be drawing to a close.

Some of the earlier buildings, as in the case of my house in York Street, are still standing – but only just! I expect it will be demolished when I pass on.

The church on Egan Street, Kalgoorlie

The Day My Cat Died

My cat was a silver grey tom, who took pleasure in entertaining the local females.

There must be something enviable about a free and easy tomcat, which arouses the ire of women in general.

My lady friends became very insistent that I get him doctored.

Finally, at their insistence and the veiled threat that they would perhaps burn my house down, the die was cast when a 'cut price' was negotiated at the vet's.

The poor cat was put into a box and consigned to his 'Executioner'.

He came back very groggy, with instructions to keep him inside for a couple of days. That I did.

A couple of days later there was no cat!

The chap next door caught me out the front at the bins and said, "You used to have a cat?"

I said, "Yes."

And he said, "It is not THAT down there?" and pointed to a mangled mite on the ground.

He said that a lady in a hysterical state had knocked on his front door saying that she had hit a cat while driving down the road. He'd had to get his wife to console the lady.

After sending the cat to 'Cat's Heaven' – the bin – I informed my friends of the cat's (alleged) suicide (in the absence of a note).

I further embellished the story by saying the cat's final act of defiance was an extended paw with a raised thumb.

My friends said I should get a refund from the vet, but I said, "I don't think it works that way."

On Mine Closures

There have been many mine closures over the years in Kalgoorlie-Boulder and surrounding Goldfields.

There are three mine closures in which I have been indirectly involved in earlier years. Nowadays mine closures usually happen in a much more planned fashion.

1. SONS OF GWALIA
2. AUSTRALIAN BLUE ASBESTOS (WITTENOOM)
3. LANCEFIELD (NEAR LAVERTON)

SONS OF GWALIA – LEONORA

I worked for three months at the Sons of Gwalia, just after I finished my apprenticeship. It was a funny old place, very rundown, but quite colourful.

I worked in the main workshop first then managed to get sent to the power station. The engines were gas-run from gas producers, in turn fed on firewood from the Woodline.

The engines would be chugging away and then the lights would go dim. Everybody (those who knew what was going on) would start rushing around like 'headless chooks' until they got it going again.

Anyway, I left in the latter part of '59 to go East with my friends.

I was in Wittenoom after my sojourn in the East. There I met fellows from Sons of Gwalia who told me the story about the mine closure.

It was around Christmas and the winder driver got drunk and pulled the skip over the top into the bin. The mine closed very soon afterwards.

AUSTRALIAN BLUE ASBESTOS – WITTENOOM

After working there for three years on and off, I left in mid '66 to go on a trip to Darwin, which ended in Perth late '66 where I learned that Australian Blue Asbestos had closed. I think the stories about Mesothelioma had a lot to do with it.

LANCEFIELD GOLD MINE

When I arrived in Kalgoorlie in '80 I had a travelling job for the Public Works Department, and I had been to Cosmo Newberry (an Aboriginal settlement) where I had been doing work on the school houses.

I had made the mistake of drinking some of the local water, which made me as 'sick as a dog', and when I got a flat on one of my truck tyres I didn't think I would get back to the Laverton Pub for the night.

A couple of prospecting-looking blokes asked me if I would like a beer. I said, "I think so". This fixed my tummy straight away.

Anyway, I had pulled up near an old mine site with chimneys, heaps of overburden and perhaps a headframe.

They told me this was the old Lancefield gold mine, reopened in the '30s by De Bernales and closed in '37 when the roof fell in, in the main drive. Luckily, nobody was underground at the time. They said that there had been 1,500 people living in the town site and that there had been ten or eleven cricket pitches in the area. Soon after this, Western mining re-opened the mine for the gold which was still underground.

Pete, the Fridgie

I was introduced to Pete by another tradie and for a time we became the 'Three Musketeers'. I was a metal worker, Pete, a fridge mechanic, and Dave, a house electrician.

Pete had a big booming voice and often didn't think what he was going to say before he said it. Pete passed away a couple of years ago and left a vacuum in Dave's and my life.

Bluff, Coolgardie

Heat

When I was young heat didn't bother me. In fact I worked through most of my summers in the Pilbara.

Wittenoom was really something. The huts we lived in were totally unlined.

This was back in days when the medical people prescribed salt, a glass of water and one salt tablet. It seemed to have a wonderful effect on me. It got rid of heat, cramps, diarrhoea, etc. Then all of a sudden the medical people flipped over and banned salt!

Edward Collick

I met Canon Edward Collick when I was seven and he was seventy-seven years of age. He was rector of St John's Anglican Church in Fremantle and I was there with my brother Peter and my mother. We two boys were about to be christened – somewhat belatedly.

Now, though I was fairly compliant, my brother announced that he 'wasn't going to let anyone sprinkle holy water on him.' It seemed as though a situation might arise similar to the one in the verse "A Bush Christening" by A. B. Paterson. However, as I remember nothing much occurred.

Rev. Edward Collick first arrived in Coolgardie in the 1890's, not long after the discovery of gold by Bayley and Ford. The town was pretty much a tent city even though the population of Coolgardie at some time then was said to be greater than Perth. Edward Collick's first congregation was small due to the fact that the males, who made up about 90% of the town, were more interested in fighting and drinking. He utilised their fighting interest and let it be known that he was prepared to fight any of these chaps, with the proviso that if he won they would be obliged to come to his tent church. Now E Collick was a very good pugilist and won most of his encounters and so increased his congregation.

Somewhere in the 1890's he performed the wedding ceremony joining my grandmother and grandfather. These two had arrived from the east as a fairly large family group and went on to establish their own dynasty in the Goldfields.

Edward Collick became an important part of Goldfields history.

People like him helped to establish an orderly community in a place which appeared not very inviting when first seen.

Edward Collick left his name on part of the Anglican Nursing home for the elderly in Kalgoorlie-Boulder.

Rae McDonald

Rae served as a Medic with NZ Army 2/1 regiment and works FIFO (Fly In, Fly Out) as a Site Supervisor with refugees. She has a degree from CSU in Social Welfare, and is currently writing a young adults' novel.

Her favourite writer is Jack Kerouac.

The Death of a Medic: My Friend

In old Burnham town I first met
A red-headed girl lest we forget
She wore boots and marched with a determined stride
With uniform a reflection of a soldier's pride
She wore a red cross on her left arm as a shield
Sent on a mission far afield

Asclepios entwined with snake and staff
She kept her patients safe from harm
For seven months she had seen
A land of desert destroyed by greed
She saw the pain beyond a young child's smile
And gave relief to aid them for a while

Honourable soldier, you fought a good fight
Your soul when it departed, detonated into the light
Your name it found fame amongst the bravest kind
My heart it cried on the day you died
We welcomed you home to a parade of tears
A goodbye not meant for your young years

I still yearn for your return
Our friendship a candle will continue to burn
For my friendship you often fought to receive
I promised you I would never leave
At the sound of the bugle as it plays the last post
At dawn I will sing you a hero's toast

Glenda (Colling) McGhee

Glenda (Colling) McGhee, Diploma of Teaching, Bachelor of Education, Northern Territory University (now Charles Darwin University).

I have worked extensively with ESOL (English Speakers of Other Languages) and NESB (Non-English Speaking Background) students both in Darwin, NT and in Bali and Jakarta, Indonesia.

My interest in writing began as a child and has developed around my time as a mother, grandmother, wife and a teacher.

When I realised that my writing interests were taking second place to other needs, I decided to seriously pursue the art of writing, so I joined the Darwin Writers' Group. For some time I enjoyed the experience of these writers.

I am currently residing with my dogs and birds in suburban Darwin where I am trying to create a tropical garden that appeals to all senses, and provides fruit, herbs and vegetables as needed for my culinary and health needs.

I will always have fond memories of my place of origin, in the Goldfields of WA.

Gold in his Veins

This story is about my recollections of my brother – a story of a boy born into a family whose ancestors had a long history of mining, both in Australia and in the old country. We were part of a big blended family of pioneering folk in the Goldfields, predominantly with Irish blood topped up with a touch of Welsh, Cornish, Scots and English blood. What a mix! But from that blend came tough, enduring people with a passion for mining that carried on throughout the subsequent generations, bringing with it mixed blessings as the miners pursued the dream of striking it rich.

My father passed on his knowledge and dreams of finding the mother lode, an elusive gold vein said to be at Gibraltar, located between Coolgardie and Bulla Bulling roadside stop and pumping station. One of my earliest and rather hazy recollections is being put in a mining bucket and winched down into my father's gold mine, which he had named after me and one of my sisters, the 'Glen-Erin'.

Nowadays, it is unlikely that very young children would be winched down into a mine pit and knowing my mother's worries as I did, I am surprised that she allowed it. That said, it was a different time when we grew up. Children had the freedom of roaming the town and outskirts of the bush, within reason. There were no organised 'play-dates', like now, in this time of intense 'stranger danger'. Everyone knew the children in the town and we minded our manners when checked by an adult.

My brother was an enterprising lad and as soon as he was able to pedal off on his bike he established a trapping run for rabbits, often setting his traps up beyond the reservoir and rising early, when it was still dark, to retrieve the rabbits he had caught. When he accompanied Great-uncle 'Jim Jar' on his fruit-and-vegie round in the town, he sold these to housewives who were able to supplement the household meat in this time when there were not any supermarkets. Our family also enjoyed many a tasty rabbit stew and at times, a bite of 'Twenty-eight'. Nowadays, I would be horrified to hear of anyone eating those beautiful green parrots but that is how it was then.

My brother was the only boy with five sisters, and was looked up to by all sisters, except when I crossed him in some way and was dealt a swift justice. I am under no false illusions about this, being fully aware that this was richly deserved though he never hit me, as some might in those tough times. This was no doubt a testament to the solid values and strength of my amazing mother.

The provocation was certainly there on the day I dared to plan a jaunt to Red Lakes, nine miles away, by bike with my faithful companion in mischief, my girlhood friend. I had a pushbike, however she did not. My plan was for her to ride my 'Flash' – so named by Dad when I desperately wanted a new bike that my parents could not afford. Dad recycled and painted 'Flash', a second-hand bike, for my Christmas gift. Never was a bike more loved and well-used.

On the day, I planned to catch my brother unawares when he returned home briefly from an outing with his mates, and take his bike. My plan worked and we sped off, no doubt chortling with glee. It was a different tale when I slunk home to face his wrath. In his anger he had swept my possessions from my dressing table. I was indignant but accepted the punishment without much noise. How foolhardy are the young, thinking little of the consequences! How lucky was I that my brother was able to rein in his anger?

In his teens, my brother had many adventures that caused my poor mother considerable worry. Not the least of these was careening through fences in bush paddocks on motor bikes and driving unregistered vehicles that he and his mates had built up from old car bodies and parts. Still, he and his mates survived intact, unlike some of the time driving 'legally' on the roads. He was truly blessed, perhaps with the luck of his Irish forebears.

As my brother grew into a young man, he applied his natural talents and studied hard. From this, he was noticed by some of the town's people and offered a mining position, at Nepean nickel mine. He continued on, combining work and study to become a mining surveyor, gaining credit in his studies and was presented with a Times Award. It was at this time that he and my father were reunited and Dad became influential in my brother's life in their pursuit of the old gold vein at Gibraltar.

In time, my brother took a risk and built up his own small company of mining and earth-moving equipment, in partnership with his brother-in-law. Together they took out a lease on the old site at Gibraltar. For some years this went well for them but unfortunately they lost the lease when the owner passed on. At a later stage, the lease was reopened and became quite successful. My brother never really recovered from this loss. Gold fever was in his veins and circumstances conspired to cheat him of the dream of finding that elusive rich gold vein at Gibraltar. My brother departed this life at far too early an age, leaving his family grief-stricken, but wiser for having known him.

Forgotten

The old crow perched precariously on the tall asbestos fence, glossy black feathers gleaming in the wintry sun, as he waited for the old man to come out with a crust of bread. A brisk breeze whipped up red dirt and blew it around the small bare backyard, leaving a faint whiff of wattle and boronia behind as the breeze moved on.

Every morning without fail the crow would wait and the old man would come out, bent over with arthritis, but always with a cheery word for Crow. This was their ritual.

Sometimes he would stumble a little if he had visitors the day before. They would commiserate their loss of friends over a bottle or two of beer. But he never forgot Crow or the other animals he cared for.

At the back of his fence there was a half 44 gallon drum filled with water for the 'roos and emus to drink from. This winter had been as dry as the seasons before it.

Then he would go out front, roll up a cigarette with his nicotine-brown stained fingers and sit on his porch, watching the blue smoke spiral slowly around before it dispersed into the dry air while he waited.

Sometimes a car from out of town would arrive and out would spill the occupants, usually adults, and occasionally some children. They would call out, "Hello Dad" or "How are you, Poppy?" and a smile would light up the old man's gnarled face.

All too soon they would depart again and the old man would go inside and close up his doors to keep the cold out. He always had a blazing fire to warm himself.

In his youth he had been a gold miner and laboured long hours with pick and shovel. His big hands still had calluses though the engrained blackness had softened with age. He had run his own show a few times but had not found the rich vein of yellow gold that he had been looking for.

The old man could turn his hand to just about anything and had when there were children to feed. It was a big family and he often worked two jobs to provide for them.

Before that he had been a stockman up north a bit. In those days he only had his Blue dog to care for. But that was before he had a family. Bluey came with him to live in the town but kept his distance from all but his master.

The old man had passed on what he knew of gold mining to his children but only his boy got caught up in the gold fever. For a time they really bonded and it warmed his heart to share his knowledge with his boy. But he was gone now and the old man buried the pain deep.

He did not find it easy to talk with his children. Like his father before him, the old man did more than he ever talked about. The love was there – if only his children recognised that. Sometimes he thought they did.

Writer's Note:

This story came to mind during a visit to my father in his later years. He had a fondness for animals and was feeding a crow daily, as well as providing water for bush animals driven in to the outskirts of town by the lack of rain. It is creative writing based on what I observed.

One More Time

I wasn't expecting it. When he came to me, he took me completely unaware. It had been so long – years – since we had last been together. Our parting had been overwhelming and very public. Saying goodbye had been difficult for me and after I cried whenever I thought about him, or saw something that reminded me of him. At that time, everything reminded me of him.

The day had started like any other day. Nothing unusual to give me warning. I was alone in the house. I turned around, perhaps alerted by his presence. And there he was. The hairs on the back of my neck prickled as his presence registered. I reached for him, forgetting the past but he did not take my hands.

"Blue, where have you been?" I cried softly. "When I read your letter, I was relieved that you were ok."

He didn't answer at first, just looked at me. Then I felt the soft brush of his presence as he drew near.

"I wrote to you before because it was time to stop grieving. Your pain was holding me here. And now I have returned to set you free from whatever ails you at this time. Let it go!"

And then he was gone, fading away as though he had never been, while tears ran down my cheeks unchecked. I knew he would never come again, but felt blessed that he had returned from beyond twice out of love for me.

Writer's Note:

I was inspired to write this story after a very dear friend died tragically. After his death I had a strange experience in which I felt as though he communicated to me. Few people believe in communication after death. My experience changed my beliefs. This is creative writing based on that communication.

Sideshow Alley

The hustle and bustle is sideshow alley.
A cacophony of sound, music blaring out,
As stall holders call, 'Step up! Step up!'
Small hands held tight, children thrust up high,
For a bird's eye view.
Pink fairy floss smearing little faces,
Spun sugar twirled, a gossamer web,
Of sticky sweet delight melting in their mouths.
Hot dogs oozing tomato sauce with mustard.
Dodge'em cars filled with proud dads and eager children,
Sweethearts snuggling up, giggling girls and brash boys,
Bumping together, with a jolt.
Merry-go-round music, as motor bikes spin,
A substitution for yester year's horses.
Ferris wheel suspended, hanging baskets rocking,
Occupants peering down on the crowd below.
The crack of rifles, metal ducks bobbing,
As one and all try their luck.
Wide-mouthed clowns swing from side to side,
Evading little balls.
The whoosh of the Octopus,
Its long arms rising and falling,
Squeals and screams of terrified delight,
In spinning Cha Cha cages,

Money, money, money, exchanging hands.
Night skies lit up by the finale of fireworks,
Sprayed pink and gold dazzle and emerald glitter trails,
Bright smiling faces, tired feet,
Happy times for all, at the Fair.

Writer's Note:

The Goldfields will always be very dear to my heart. I come from pioneering families who settled there in the very early days of settlement. I grew up on the Goldfields, married and had my first child there. There are many memories to draw on. One of these was the Goldfields Fair. This prose was inspired by my impressions of the highlights of the Fair.

Donnie Martin

I came to Kalgoorlie in the Goldfields towards the end of 2007, taking up a new job and seeking adventure after working and raising a family of three in Adelaide, South Australia, for some years. I was trepidatious about the heat and at the time I imagined staying here for perhaps two years, but it is now twelve years later. I have found the Goldfields incredibly beautiful; I love the trees and the vast distances, the old buildings and the people. Sadly my husband died a couple of years ago but in a way that enabled me to stay here longer, although I expect to return to Adelaide where my children are sometime in the future. I'm fascinated by Goldfields history and the woodlands, enjoy time in the bush, taking photos, and taking part in local activities like art exhibitions, writing competitions and choir performances. As a child I loved reading and went on to study English language and literature at University. I've always loved playing with words and now find it much easier to write for fun, without the severe censoring of youth and academia. For me Kalgoorlie and the Goldfields are full of hidden treasures, waiting to be experienced and described.

Goldfields Moon

Life in her hands, as moon is held by night,
Its radiance spilling over edge of dusky land,
Swells large in desert sky, growing into sight,
Soft beams of light through gimlet trees are fanned.
She gazes on that glowing golden moon
As it takes its path though stars in myriads bright
Thinking on the ones who left too soon
Their lives cut short, it isn't right.
Their spirits crowd around her in the air
Calling come to us, join us here.
A choice too easy, leave this wearisome world,
By darkest night in black the soul is called.
    Moon holds her captured in its steady glow
    The voice within says not yet time to go.

Thunderstorm

It had been hot for days – but a change was coming. Clouds were starting to build and in the distance you could hear a deep-throated rumble.

Harney and June stood out the back, staring at the sky, both wondering how much longer they could hang on. So hot, so dry, the vegies hung limp and the chooks had stopped laying long since.

"Might make a brew," said June. "You gonna tie up that dog of yours? He'll be off when that storm breaks."

She heard him mumble: "Bloody nuisance anyway, might as well let him go, before I have to shoot him."

Silly old coot, she thought; *he loves that dog, more than me likely*. She turned inside, wondering for the umpteenth time what they were going to do.

Back in her stifling kitchen June hauled sticks out of the wood box and poked the fire. Most of their neighbours had gone – caught that train out when the mine closed all of a sudden. But she and Harn stayed, past making a new life for themselves. Sometimes, not very often, they'd get a letter from Bob, telling how well he was doing in Perth. No place for us though, Harn would say.

June emptied tea leaves on the dusty geraniums out the front of their corrugated iron cottage, a shack really. The lightning was flickering closer now, over the bare hill. *At least we might get a bit of rain out of it*, she thought.

'Come on, Harn," she called. "Come under the porch before it pours and have your cuppa."

As soon as they sat down the storm broke over their heads with a blinding flash. Thunder crashed straight after. June saw the old dog come flying past like a mad thing and then, as another fork of lightning electrified the air, he bolted, howling down the track towards the mine.

Heavy drops of rain plonked into the dust out of the black sky. Harney looked in the direction his dog had disappeared. June thought, *what did I tell you, silly old bugger, next thing you'll be going looking for him.*

Harn pulled on his old coat against the pelting rain. "Better go after him I s'pose," he said, without looking at her.

"Watch your feet," said June, "or you'll be down one of them holes for sure." She stared after him as he started down the track in the rain.

Not much she could do, at least the bit of a garden would get a soaking; if it wasn't all washed away.

June sat on the porch watching water pool around the house and run down the path, and wondered what Bob would be doing right now. Proud of her boy she was, and missed him. Then an idea occurred to her. What if Harn did fall down a hole? What if the dog never came back and neither did he? What if he couldn't be found?

Guess she'd just have to pack everything up and move: she'd done it before.

June sat in the dark, a slow smile coming to her face.

A Small Earthquake

It's hard to find the words to describe an earthquake. We had a little one the other day, Valentine's Day actually. When my daughter rang later I tried to describe the sensation, but it was hard to convey the oddly disturbing feeling it aroused, especially when it wasn't very big. Three point something I heard later. We get a few of these small tremors in Kalgoorlie, not like the big one in 2010.

When it happened it was just on 6.15 am. The morning seemed sunny, bright and peaceful. I'd just settled down to my morning cup of tea when there was a strange sound, a kind of crack or bang within the house. Then it was followed by a disturbance in the air, a movement through the rooms, like a wind or something rushing through from front to back. Last, a rumbling noise that went on for quite a while, and could have been mistaken for a train on the nearby tracks. But somehow everything felt strange, and I stared out the window, expecting an answer, to see something changed. The trees, the sky, the houses, all looked the same, only the air felt different.

It would be easy to imagine that a spirit was abroad, and if anything fell down you might say it was a poltergeist.

Goldilocks and the Three Thieves

Once upon a time there was a little girl named Goldilocks who lived in a small cottage with her family.

They had a wonderful orchard which Goldilocks looked after every day. Many different citrus trees thrived in the sunny climate of the Goldfields where the family lived. There were oranges, grapefruit, mandarins, lemons and even cumquats. The people of the Goldfields liked the look of these tiny fruit, but not the taste. They were far too sour.

One day when Goldilocks went to the orchard she saw some of the oranges had been eaten. The skins remained hanging from the trees but the flesh was gone. Goldilocks said crossly, "Who's been eating my oranges?"

No one answered because there was no one there.

The next day Goldilocks saw some of the lemons had been eaten. Half eaten lemons lay around under the trees. This was too much. She stamped her foot in annoyance and disappointment.

That night she vowed to hide in the orchard to see who was eating the fruit. She climbed into a tall tree and waited.

After a while she heard rustling noises, and in the light of the moon she could see a large furry possum creeping along a branch towards a big orange. Next she noticed a smaller possum coming along behind. Suddenly she shone her torch on the procession. In the torchlight she could see a tiny baby possum clinging to its mother's fur. Although all three looked very cute, Goldilocks needed to protect her fruit so she spoke sternly; "You can't eat this fruit. It's not yours!"

To her surprise the possum said, "But we have to feed our baby!"

Quick as a flash Goldilocks said, "You can have all the cumquats you like, as long as you leave the rest."

At that the possums ran away into the night, but from that time on, only the cumquats were eaten.

Vigil

I was in a deep, deep sleep, floating in a sea of dreams, then, suddenly BANG! I was awake.

Fear engulfed me. Eyes wide open, heart lurching, instantly alert, I took in the scene. The dim lighting, the monitor in the corner, the shape on the bed, tubes and wires in all directions.

Voices from outside the room, not important, dismissed. A noise from the figure on the bed, hoarse rasping sounds. What was happening? Was this the moment?

How long had I been asleep, minutes, hours? Had I fallen asleep when I should have been watching? Last night he'd wanted to talk; reminiscing about times with his brothers and sisters; how they stayed up late chatting when they were supposed to be asleep. Exhausted I'd lain down on the cloud chair, specially designed for patient comfort and rest, but lately my haven for the long nights of keeping vigil.

I was out of that high cloud chair in a flash, stiffness from the awkward lying forgotten, reaching his side. His hands were lifted from the sheets, almost waving, eyes shut, still breathing. Still there, still with us. I tried to slow my breathing, stay calm, stay in control, he was relying on me.

I stared at the monitor that I'd come to love and hate over the past days, telling us the moment by moment story of oxygen, blood pressure, temperature. We'd learnt what to look for, knowing that even as he started to feel cooler from the ice packs and fans, that the screen showed his temperature crawling upwards inexorably and ominously once again. Knowing we were on borrowed time.

A nurse hurried in, alarmed by the noises from the bed. She looked at him, looked at me.

"Is he in pain? I can get morphine."

"No," I said. I knew what that meant.

"No," I said, realisation dawning, "He's singing, singing along to his IPod."

I leaned closer to make out the words.

"…you were always on my mind, you were always on my mind."

Singing along to Elvis, at this time of extremity? What was he thinking? Was he afraid too; seeking comfort in the power of that great voice?

I took his hand. His eyes opened; he had a small smile on his lips. Each moment a lifetime. I realised he was sending a message. For now my fear subsided to a dull ache. I smiled back.

Brian Nazzari

I am a husband and father of four. I recently retired from the workforce. I have always liked to write rhyming poems. Some of the poems in the book were written a number of years ago. My first poems (in the book) were written to fill the gap left by an empty house, when the children grew up and left home and Kalgoorlie for University. My Prospector poem referred to a gold prospector on the Goldfields; a lifelong interest for me, most of my family and also my brother-in-law (dec'd). It is a hobby pursued by many Goldfielders, especially in earlier days.

Two old prospectors, Len and Bluey

Goldman

He was the true bushman and prospector,
Yes, the bush's unofficial inspector,
Gold sat heavily on his mind,
Every day brought hope of a new find.

Detecting every inch of ground,
Just waiting for the right sound,
Wasn't much he didn't know about this game
He had some good strikes and a little fame.

Walking miles and miles in unforgiving heat,
Checking those tired, swollen and blistered feet,
He reckons it's not too bad today,
He has a half an ounce of gold for pay.

Loaming will be the go tomorrow,
This can come with heartache and sorrow,
Looking for the big Mother Lode,
He's using all his skills to crack the code.

A lot of sweat and hard toil
The reef is exposed from the soil
You won't hear him scream and shout
Well then tomorrow's another day
With prospecting that's just the way.

The Reason Why?

Time drifts slowly on by.
Cool wind blowing pretty blue sky.
I watch as healthy birds fly,
Then I wonder why, why, why?

We are put here for a reason,
It's not just someone teasing,
Many thoughts going through my mind.
The reason I can't seem to find.

Then life doesn't always explain,
I find that a damned shame.
So I just keep on wondering why?
As I watch the healthy birds fly by.

Maybe I am here to provide and do good?
Or maybe I'm here just to cut the wood?
Maybe I am here to cherish and love?
I don't know; there are no signs from above.

I am left on this lonely perch,
My brain is going to have to research,
There must be many a reason,
Not just to experience the season.

Then maybe one day I'll find out,
What this life is all about,
Whether or not it has been worthwhile,
And I satisfy myself with a little smile.

Give Us a Call on the Phone

Give us a call on the phone,
Don't feel miserable and all alone.
You don't have to bottle things up inside,
We are always here and we tried.
Yeah, tried to let you have a say,
Of all your problems facing you today,
Bring it all out into the open,
You'll find it's a fine way of coping.
We know better than the average folk,
We know it's serious and not a joke,
You can speak to us quite freely,
Because we love you so dearly
There isn't a thing we don't understand,
That is why parents are so grand,
You can rest your mind at ease,
We always aim to please.
Then after our little chit chats,
You'll realise we're a pair of 'smart cats,'
Afterwards you'll feel real happy and gay,
And it's only the phone call you'll have to pay.
We love you more than we can say,
That has always been our way.
We wait eager to hear the ring.
We'll be here to do our thing.

The Kiddies Are Gone

The Kiddies are gone
The noise was so loud it could burst your eardrums
The kids all studying, learning their sums
Cooking smells erupting out of the stove
Clothes flapping from the clothesline by the drove
Sitting around the table debating most events
Children ready to go out smelling of different scents
Discussions of the new love in their lives
When or when not they may become wives
Laughing, smiling, crying, happiness and joy
Screaming, teasing, fighting even with the boy
Sad times, bad times and the good times
And the rich and fruitful times when we had dimes
Now a deadly silence has fallen on the house
You could hear the movement of a mouse
The flock have all flown the nest
I sit at the table thinking in my old vest.
Now it is just my wife and me
All the kids live down by the sea (nearly)
We'd give anything to have them back home

A Daughter's Response to Dad

Poems about war
Or love lost – or never found –
Can be sad
But not always
As sad
As a poem about a garden, or a house
Or a family
Your family
That knocks you for six
So when you're reading
Tears well up in your eyes
And you think of
Your old Dad
Sitting at the kitchen table,
With or without his vest,
Thinking …
And you wish you could
Go home
To rescue or be rescued?
But you know you can't –
At least not for a while –
So far away,
Near the sea
And it gets you
Thinking …
Because I live near the sea

Exchange Hotel
Corner of Maritana and Hannan Streets. Kalgoorlie

Lesley Nazzari

I grew up in Coolgardie, but moved to Kalgoorlie to marry Brian. I have been in Kalgoorlie for over 46 years. We had four children. – three girls and a boy.

I have always enjoyed stories and reading. It wasn't until my children were grown up that I began to write again. I was involved in a writing group while I was doing a Humanities course in 2000 at Kalgoorlie College/Curtin University.

I like to 'make things.' I sewed and knitted in earlier days. Later on, I tried various art forms at Kalgoorlie College for a number of years. I completed an Associate Degree in Art 2001-2.

I have run the Goldfields Writing Group for about 4 years.

Bella

Bella

She is Black and Tan
Her eyes are liquid brown pools
Yard is a war zone

(Bella has made our middle ground, yard, look like war zone)

Bella

Black Dog

A walk for black dog
She is asleep peacefully
War zone tomorrow

"Cringe"/'Christine' Goes Missing

It was just an ordinary day. Anna and Ryan were going off to town early.

We had just finished breakfast when Anna came back with the sad news that her car 'old Christine' was missing.

'Christine' was nowhere to be seen. She was usually sitting sedately up on the front footpath.

"Anna, you must ring the police," I said, puzzled. It was an old car, who would steal it?

And she did! This was testament to her surprise and annoyance at 'Christine's' disappearance.

Neither of my younger children liked to make phone calls when they were young.

After this was done Ryan and Anna set off to town. They walked at a brisk pace until they arrived at the library, which was, and is only a few blocks away.

And 'Lo and behold' there was 'Christine' parked at the front of the library.

They ran home to get the keys.

But on the way home Anna's mind was 'ticking over', and by the time she arrived back home she was very angry.

"Mum, you took 'Christine' to the library and forgot to bring her home."

I had no memory of doing any such thing. But after a while it all began to fall into place and I could see that she was right!

It was my habit to walk to the library, but I had driven this time because I had 'stuff' on my mind. And in my preoccupied state I had walked home and forgotten the car.

I can smile now when I write this story. It was not always so.

For years the story of ‘how mum lost a car’ was ‘trotted out’ on all family occasions. I hated the story with a passion.

Even my friends, who were quite kind, were forced on occasion to tell the story of ‘Christine’ when there was a lull in the conversation.

Lost and Found

I was a young mother and had all my children in quick succession. Looking back on those days, I wonder how I managed. I am sure it was difficult, but manage I did.

I didn't drive in those days and I used to walk to town with a pram which had a little seat for a toddler. My youngest child and the toddler were pushed in the pram. My four-year-old walked too. No wonder she loves running and exercise now.

It was quite a walk. It takes ten to fifteen minutes from our street to the centre of Kalgoorlie. The walk didn't worry me at the time; I did it frequently. Perhaps I caught a taxi home. My memory is no longer clear.

What I do remember is one time being in Hannan Street with my baby in the pram and my two other little girls, I was about eight months pregnant with my final child, a boy (but I didn't know that at the time). I can remember being in a shop called Hamilton's, a clothing store. It was around about where 'Echo' has been for a number of years now.

I can't remember what I was looking for at the time. The store was packed with lots of clothes and had a big floor space. It was rather a jumbled and overstocked store in those days as I recall.

After a short time it came to my attention that my little girl, Mel, was missing. She had completely disappeared. I looked everywhere for her.

I have a memory of walking up and down Hannan Street, crying my eyes out. I had on a black dress with coloured roses on it. I am not sure why this has stayed in my mind, maybe it was because I had few clothes that fitted by then, and I had worn it often. However, despite my tears, Mel was nowhere to be found. I kept a firm grip on my eldest girl and the pram with the baby.

Normally Mel would have been sitting on the little seat on the pram. I must have let her down in the shop, as she was no doubt tired of being restricted in the seat.

I should have known what would happen, as Mel had a habit of running the other way when she was tired or bored, but I didn't expect her to disappear so quickly.

Eventually, I was forced to go the Police Station to report to them that my child was lost. It transpired that a nice man had taken Mel to the Police Station and there she was, sitting down having milk and biscuits with the constabulary.

She was a friendly child, so she probably enjoyed the attention at the time.

I was very relieved to see that she was ok and safe.

We were so lucky that the story had a happy ending.

House Fire

My secret fear is being caught in a house fire, or any fire for that matter.

This fear is not unfounded because I actually have experienced the terror of such a fire. Our house was severely damaged by fire about 32 years ago.

The damage was difficult to cope with, and resulted in us living in a caravan for about three months while the house was repaired. We could have two of our children in the caravan with us, but due to lack of space, two children had to live with their aunt for this period of time.

However, the most frightening aspect of that night was that we could have all been burnt to death.

As it was, my eldest daughter awoke with the smell of smoke at about 2 am in the morning and called, “Mum, I can smell smoke.”

Luckily I heard her and I could also smell smoke. I tried to rouse my husband: he opened his eyes and looked at me, but did not get up. Unfortunately, I did not realise this immediately. I was intent on hustling the children out of the house.

Standing by the dividing fence I screamed out to Dominic, our next door neighbour, to ring the Fire Brigade. Flames were leaping out of the house by now.

Hubby gave one terrible yell, “Lal!”

I tried to go back inside but the smoke would not allow me to enter again. I did not know at the time that smoke rises and I could have crawled back inside.

The Fire Brigade arrived and were able to break the bedroom window and rescue hubby, who was unconscious by that time. He was taken to hospital in an ambulance and was brought around.

I remember that they asked him about his football team. It was

East Fremantle at the time. They had won that day, consequently Bri had partaken of a few ales.

Thankfully he was ok and was able to come home from hospital after a few days.

We had family and community help, and a donation from the Fire Brigade. We also had house insurance, which enabled us to get the house rebuilt (in the damaged area, and repainted throughout). Sadly, the part that was completely destroyed was our girl's bed room that had only just been built on to the house not too long before the fire.

The fire was a shock, but we were able to get back on our feet, in time.

However, I felt compelled to feel the walls for heat for many years after the fire. The fire had originated from our lounge room open fireplace.

We had a good fire going that day. It was the 18th of May, I can recall the date, but not the year. My eldest child was twelve. It was a cold winter day.

I was reminded of the house fire just recently when a bin at my work caught fire. I was alerted by the heat that was coming into the doorway. When I looked out I saw smoke and flames. In no time at all flames were leaping into the air and the green rubbish bin melted in a fascinatingly awful manner.

My co-worker managed to put the fire out with a nearby garden hose, so it ended well. However, it was a reminder of the savage power of fire.

Bindi's Shame

A small warm body
A grey bundle of feathers
She breathes no more.

The naughty culprit
Comes running, tail wagging
'Wicked girl' I say.

Homeless Man

His chosen place of rest; a church
Not inside, but on the porch.
Not much cover from the weather,
And all alone, not together
No friend to share the dark of night,
How did he come to this sad plight?

At first glance a lump of old rags,
Head propped up against the crags.
I wonder how he can sleep away
When sun is up to greet the day
The heat must soon cause him to leave,
I trust he doesn't have to thieve.

What does he do all day? I think
Someone will soon create a 'stink'.
Like clockwork he is back at night.
Does he take a fright or flight?
We notice as we drive abroad,
He holds a coffee like a Lord.

(I was inspired to write about the homeless man, after seeing an old man on the street each day as we drove into town. It made me think about his life and then construct a possible story for him.)

Bulla Bulling

As an outlying place to the Goldfields, Bulla Bulling plays a part in my early memory. There is nothing much there except a pub, a road (the main highway to Perth) and a granite outcrop which is located back a little way from the pub.

Alongside of the highway the rail runs, or it used to. I don't think it does these days. I don't remember seeing Bulla Bulling on our recent and frequent trips to Perth by train. And running parallel to the rail line was the pipeline that provided, and still provides, much needed water to the Goldfields and other little towns along the way.

Bulla Bulling was one of my father's favourite places to visit when we were quite young children. He had various vehicles in his life-time, but the one that has fixed itself firmly in my mind is a green van. I think the colour was British Racing Green, and it had probably been a delivery van in an earlier life. Anyway, on a sudden whim, we would all be piled into the van and driven to 'Bulla', as it was commonly known.

In those days the pub at Bulla was owned and run by Mario and Maria. Mario was a jovial and chunky Italian immigrant along with his tiny Italian wife, Maria. At that time, when I was about six or seven years old, I think Maria could only speak Italian.

Apart from the 'Rock Hotel', the other attraction at Bulla was my father's bachelor brothers who worked for the water supply and lived across the road and railway line in little Water Supply huts. Dad thought very highly of his brothers judging by the way he talked. The brothers were known respectively as Muzza and Moggie. I am unsure why but the nicknames seemed to suit them. I was too young to know what their jobs involved, but I imagine that perhaps this was where one of the pumping stations was, and that was why they were there. Anyway, going to Bulla to see the uncles seemed exciting and mysterious when we were young.

I have several vague memories of one such trip, or perhaps I have merged the memories now, as it is over 50 years ago. The uncles were good sorts as I understood then and later. They loved a drop of ale but always kept themselves clean and respectable. In later years when they moved to Coolgardie they could often be seen on Saturday mornings walking off to the Denver City Hotel in dark pants and white shirts. Of course, I never saw them on their homeward journey, but pride was important to them, so I imagine they were still looking reasonably good.

The first memory of visiting the uncles is of the Uncles listening to the cricket. There was no TV in those days. My father always listened to the test matches too. Uncle Mog had been, and may have still been at that time, a very good fast bowler. Many years later, when asked if Muz was also a good cricketer, Mog replied, 'Mmm … he thought he was." Roy was always 'quick off the mark' with his comments.

The other memory was of my brother and me running along the pipeline, unsure if our sisters were old enough to do this too. The pipeline seemed to have a bigger circumference in those days.

Many trips we had to Bulla in those days. I remember Mario and Maria quite fondly and also the uncles. They are all safely tucked away in my memory, as I saw them then, through a child's eyes.

Pioneer Newly Weds

The wedding was over,
The shadows grew long,
The tired dray rattled on,
Like them it was strong.
But it had been a long day.

When finally they stopped
In space, naturally cleared
Of the tall and looming gums
No house nor hearth appeared
And it had been a long day.

New wife glanced at husband
Softly, brown eyes asking;
'The house? Is it far from here?'
He grunted, eyes downward, masking.
It had been such a long day.

'It's packed on the dray
And needs to be erected."
And she, tough lady, set to work
As he undoubtedly expected.
A long day, turning now to night.

No tears or tantrums
Here they'd do no good.
She knew this pioneer man
Had heart of stone and wood
It would be a long night.

But 'fore long he lit a fire
And got the billy bubbling
He pointed at two dusty swags
And dark became less troubling.
A long day ending.

"Tonight we'll sup our tea
And 'neath the stars we'll sleep.
Tomorrow there'll be time for tents
And building something we can keep."
A new day begins.

The 'old camp' had appeared

LESLEY NAZZARI – COLLING WALK FREMANTLE TO COOLGARDIE

Her boots had sprung holes,
But she kept on going.
With brother ahead,
There'd be no slowing.
Despite their weariness

The old wagon swayed,
And rumbled along the track,
Carrying the father's new bride,
There'd be no turning back
Despite the distance

Days and weeks had passed,
Walking on through the heat,
They battled insects, dust and flies,
And now and then sleet.
Despite their pain

Tom harboured a dream,
Which he enjoyed while walking,
The dream was of a gold nugget
He'd heard them all talking,
Despite their secrecy

At night they made camp.
And he filled the pot,
With food he had hunted
And very likely shot.
Despite the darkness

There was very little water,
On the trip east to the 'fields.
Tom eked out their share each day,
Only so much his waterbag could yield.
Despite the worry

Sticky flies hovered around
Their eyes with each mile,
But on they continued,
Then Tom's lips formed into a smile.
Despite the odds

He still hoped to strike it very rich
Now his job for his father was done
Bride and daughters safely delivered
He grabbed his pick and started a ditch
Despite the failure of others

He may not have struck gold
But he passed the longing
And the pleasure in the quest
On to his many Colling descendants
Despite the pain and work

Note:

This prose was written after reading an old newspaper article telling about Tom Colling, Dad's father and his siblings, (ages ranging from eight to twenty five years), arrival to Coolgardie, in the Goldfields by foot from the Fremantle port. They were guided by John Lewis Colling, their older brother and accompanied by their Stepmother who travelled in her small cart with their belongings. The journey took four weeks and it took the Colling siblings three weeks to recover from the difficult journey.

Ryan Nazzari

I have always liked to write and was involved with a Writing Group when I lived in Kalgoorlie and was attending Curtin University where I did a bridging course. Later I moved to Perth to complete my Fine Arts Degree, and also an extra year for Honours, Curtin University, Bentley. Painting is my first love. I spent a number of years doing art related subjects at Kalgoorlie College before it became a part of Curtin University.

Old Man

Landed old man
Distance and your skin are marked
Aged
Older than me
But I felt this tide between us go in and out
What Fathers don't say to sons?
What words can be spoken alone by you and me
We are blood kin
Tied forever.

We are so much

We are so much
And yet
Little exchanges
Are often the most profound
The most telling of our character.
How many people
Live in one body
At any given moment?

Re-painting

New skin
Old painting
Life lived in layers
Like a painting
A hundred hidden dreams

Family Thoughts & Granddad

Across the sky the crows fly
Like dark cut out poppet headed wheels
They voice their history
The dry bark of my childhood
And early morning waking in dust.

In red dust
In the golden rays of my mother
In the sharp silver flares of my father
In the diamond shine of my three sisters

Children grow and leave
Become the world
The world is deaf and dumb
But in the early dark hours
You revisit youth.

You revisit youth and love
Youth and failings too
I wish on dreams. I am made of confused smoke
From backyard parties and lemon cheesecake.

Where is the harbour and mooring for such time?
Pouring coloured water onto a plastic sheet
In neat wells
A line of red
A line of green
And a line of blue.

But the memories become murky puddles. Colours and thoughts and thinking flood into one another.

I remember before my grandad died we went to see him in his little Pension flat in Coolgardie.
Where he enjoyed showing my mother and me
the crows he had been feeding
At his back fence.
It seems a dream now.
A strange considered sunset.

We always miss family
We always miss blood.

Field naturalists exploring Caenyie Rock, near Wallaroo

Jenni Needham

Jenni is a young writer who came along to the group for several years. She enjoys writing; the challenge of using her imagination to create another world and be totally immersed in her writing until it is complete to her satisfaction. Jenni also wrote Fan Fiction. She works in a local retail store.

Lake Perkolilli, Kurnalpi

Susie Sung the Blues

On a hot steamy night
Susie sung the Blues
For the people's delight
Susie sung the Blues
With all her might
For early in her life
She was once just a wife

Remembrance

A straight line is formed
Everybody is saluting
They look like real life soldiers
Posing for a timeless picture
They are made to have ghostly appearances
There's an Airforce pilot
A Nurse
A Doctor
An Army Officer
A Navy Officer
A Reporter/Photographer
A Reserve Officer
A Housewife and House Husband
A Parent
An Engineer
A Mechanic
An Intelligence Officer
A Resistance fighter
A Miner
A Recruiter
A Messager [Cableman]
A General
A Soldier
A Horse
A Dog
A Veteran
A Factory worker
A Prisoner of War

A Monument Man
A Politician
A Lover
A Parent
A Child
Death

A sign above them has a stop insignia; with Anzac colours painted on it
It reads 'STOP AND REMEMBER'
These men and women are all from different cultures, backgrounds, religions, walks of life
But they come together and stand united to represent theirs and our beloved country;
They fight for Freedom, Families, Friends, Community, Change;
Not just for ours but theirs too
For the strangers standing next to them
'LEST WE FORGET'!

Sand plain near Mt Burges

Gudrun Charlotte Sahm

Born and educated in Germany, I completed my Master in Dressmaking in Hanover when it was convenient with my four children.

A few years after my husband's death, I moved to Australia with my new partner.

In 1986 we came to the Goldfields.

Since I had the opportunity to study at the Kalgoorlie College, together with Edith Cowen University, it has opened another door in life for me and is a great challenge.

I made my Associate Degree in Visual Arts with Edith Cowen University in 1997.

Now I am in the Golden Mile Art Exhibition Group and make paintings, drawings, linocuts, collographs and etchings.

Every year I have some of my Art in the Kalgoorlie /Boulder Art prize and the Members' exhibition. One of my paintings is in Berlin (Art on the Move) in the Museum of Checkpoint Charlie.

I was involved in many other Exhibitions, had two Exhibitions on my own in Germany, two in the Arts Centre, Kalgoorlie, two in Kalgoorlie Galleries and several in the Arts House from the GMAEG.

I also published a book, *The Tree and I*, in a German and English version with a book opening in Germany and in the Boulder Art House.

A Trip to Burra Rocks

When you drive through the bush around Coolgardie there are many stunning places to find. One day we drove out towards Burra Rocks with some friends. As we were slowing down and looking which way to go, an emu decided to run next to us. My friend had the window open and the emu put his head in. My husband was the driver and drove very slowly but the emu was going the same speed. Then he drove a bit faster, the emu ran faster as well, it was hopeless, so he slowed down again. In the end the emu parted from us down a side track. We were happy that he was unhurt and now we could enjoy the beautiful landscape around us. That was the first part of the adventure.

Then we came to Burra Rocks and enjoyed the picturesque view. It was a lovely day. We snapped on our bathers and went halfway up the rock. There is a water catchment and it was just what we needed, so refreshing! Little fish were swimming with us so there was also something to watch. Later we went up to the top, and had the most enjoyable view. Nothing disturbed our outlook. There are big boulders; they looked like huge creatures. You would think they might roll down at any moment, but no, they stayed still and didn't do us any harm.

When we came down we had a sausage sizzle on the BBQ; we had earned it. After a little walk down around the base of the rock we went home; we were very tired. We had such a good day.

My Special Colour

Thinking about colours is interesting, but when it comes to decide which one is my beloved colour then I get confused. Definitely I love red in all shades from a lofty light red to dark, nearly purple. If I want to lighten up my day, I definitely get a red shirt out of the cupboard; it just feels good and makes the day bright.

But then, when I look at the sky, I think what a lovely blue is there, it means so much to us; it brings the new day into position. Also, blue is a colour for queens and kings and King's blue is stunning especially when it is on velvet. Not to forget the blue flower. She brings fairy tales to us, she has a perfume, and she looks beautiful. She has healing power. Has she really healing power? Maybe not, but what does it matter? She brings joy to us!

So there, we are not a hundred percent behind the red.

And it gets worse! The sunny yellow comes along! Thinking of Van Gogh's sun flowers lets my soul sing; what a yellow! These shiny, warm tones are like music; they lift you up! The sun itself gives us light. What is a day without light? It brings us down. And there is the golden shine of candles in the Old Dutch paintings. What a sensation it brings to the picture, fields of ripe grain, bending over in the wind, another yellow. This one is very important because it brings food which we all need.

The whole rainbow is absolutely wonderful; every colour in it has a different outlook and meaning. We need them all; otherwise our life is bleak and gloomy. So let us enjoy the wonderful rainbow, not only as colours but also in our life.

I left out white and black. They also have their place, because they underline the colours, make them glow and give them the right company.

Lost in the Music

Music comes in different varieties, so everybody can find pleasure in listening to their special assortment.

I myself love many different sorts of music. I like to sing along, or whistle when I do something.

For years and years the Don Cossacks came to our city, and every year we went and listened to their songs. Most of the Cossacks were the survivors from the Tsar's troops who fought against the Russian Revolution. They came together with Serge Jaroff and built a choir which had the compassion like musical instruments. As we went into our beautiful theatre, every place was occupied. The people loved the Russian songs.

The bell rang. All was quiet. The curtain opened. The Cossacks stood there in a half circle, all in black, loose shirts, trousers and shiny, soft, long boots. Hanging from each of their belts was a diamante cross, blinking in the shine of the stage lights. And now Serge Jaroff came in, a tiny man against the others, but what a personality! He went into the middle, stepped up two steps and the music began.

This choir could take us emotionally up and down; their songs were filled with emotion; they used their voices like instruments, they shouted, whispered, laughed, and brought their stories to us; we didn't need an interpreter.

The Cossack patrol is most impressive; it begins with a faraway stamping sound of horses hoofs, first very gentle, it comes nearer and nearer and the music gets louder, then it's next to you, loud, frolicsome, full of life; they sing, they whistle, they ride at full gallop; stamping hoofs are clapping. Then it is over, the noise fades away to a whisper.

The Evening Bells tell the story about the end of the working day; people are on their way home from the fields. They enjoy the peaceful twilight and the last song of a bird; the speed of the working day is over. The song begins very softly with deep tunes, then a Tenor brings it to higher levels and the choir joins in with a romantic sound, telling the day's story. The evening church bell ends with one very high tune, but the choir is in deep sound. It takes you away in different spheres; the world around isn't important anymore; it is such a good feeling!

The bell is ringing; it is the celebration of the peaceful evening. The bell tells you the church is open, come. In the old Russian church, bells were a big part of their lives, as it was in our country in earlier times and still is in small communities.

How did they do it? Serge Jaroff placed all the equal voices together in lines. Nearly all of them were able to sing on their own, and that's what they were doing in turns. They sang a bit then the choir joined in, then again another one, some very deep, so your hair stood up, some were very high and fine like singing glass, or, of course, different bells.

Some stories are very dramatic, like Stena Rasin. Other stories are very powerful, like The Wolga Schlepper. And there is the lovely song, Kalinka. But there are also songs which go with clapping and laughter and whistling.

I, for my part, never went away from a concert like that without tears in my eyes, not only because of sadness, but also because I was happy. It brought so many feelings up.

Australia Day

Australia Day brings up lovely memories. The last one was a big breakfast in the Centenary Park and it was lovely to see all the happy faces around. The Rotary Club had a lot to do, but they all enjoyed doing it and created a wonderful atmosphere. The music played Australian songs, some groups danced, new citizens were announced, stalls had something to sell or made their group known, and the place was full of colour and laughter.

Then my thoughts went back to our earlier years in the Goldfields, when this was all very new to us. It will never be like that again, because then it was just Kalgoorlie, a town, not a city, so it was more personal and intimate. It was happening at the outside swimming pool, which is long closed and rotting away. This swimming pool was absolutely beautiful! It had an Olympic pool to swim in but also a wonderful waterway running towards a relaxing little pond, not only for children, just for all the family. Sitting in the grassy area of the swimming pool was just lovely, there was enough shade from the trees and the water course helped to cool one down.

On Australia Day they had lots of tables and chairs around. The Mayor made the speeches, he introduced the new citizens, and after this he went from one table to the next and talked to everyone: he was a lovely man.

He would ask us all where we came from, and ask us if we like the Goldfields, and then he would tell us it was a good life in this region and so on. At this time I was studying at Kalgoorlie College, this was one of his 'Love Childs', so we had something in common. He was also the Mayor who was behind the Art Centre, which brought culture to the Goldfields, and we still enjoy the exhibitions and events in this important building.

This water splashing Australia Days sits in my memory as a good part of my life in Australia.

Grass tree near Mt Burges

Eugene Winter

I'm 75 years old, born and educated in Germany, self-employed in Germany, travelled the world, worked a few years in Nigeria, Saudi Arabia and some other European countries. My family lives in the USA where I have been several times, and sailed a few years on cargo ships and oil tankers around the world. I had a lot of assignments as Engineer and Manager.

I migrated to Australia; stayed in Adelaide. I had my Private Pilot Licence and extended Aerobatic Licence. While self-employed in Adelaide I travelled to see more of Australia, and made my home in Coolgardie where I now live. I have a partner of 39 years and we are very lucky to be together this long span of life. In return, to give something back to Australia, I became Justice of the Peace in 1996 and was twice elected Councillor of the Shire of Coolgardie.

Music is Emotional and Full of Sound

The first cry of life brings joy to the heart
Of the mother when a child enters the world.
It is the beginning of a journey through space and time.
It is like boarding a train with many stations, stops and starts;
With people enjoying the same journey for a while and becoming friends;
People leaving and continuing their journey to another place.
We hear the sound of wheels from the carriage over the rail,
ratata, ratata, ratata.
It sounds like a melody, which we truly adore and our spirits soar like an eagle over the hill
Mozart lets our souls vibrate and touches our heart, and we can't help but smile
Pavarotti clearly enlightens our day with his 'Nesum Dorma' and makes us feel happy in many ways.
Music is our own experience, giving expression to our thoughts and giving our soul wisdom.
Since the beginning of time there is mathematics in the scale of tones, and music in the space of spheres.
Music is an emotional statement which expresses the inner self
Listen to the sound around you. Listen to the tweeting of the birds.
If you understand them you will understand the spiritual ego, yourself.

A bird can sing a wonderful song in the morning, without knowing if it will be dead by the setting of the sun.

Death will come one day when we don't know; but there will be lots of singing.

When we leave this wonderful life and arrive at the golden gates with the great sound of angels.

"Please come in weary wanderer
You have done your lot, and
It is time to rest your soul."

The Trees Bear the Age of a Forgotten Time

Imagine the images of mystery and intrigue of what life was like back in the days when hundreds or even thousands of people resided there, and what the chain of events were that led to it becoming deserted.

The mere mention of a ghost town is often enough to pique the interest in haunted houses, because they conjure images of such mystery and intrigue.

The swirling wind hovers over the leaves and releasing the voices of the hesternal (*relating to yesterday*).

Passing over the graveyard of the long forgotten town which was bustling with life.

It is long gone, but shines the light on the living as the ray of sun reveals the mystery of an antecedent (*history, ancestors*) event.

The wind lets you feel the agonising, the hardship of our ancestors in the rush to dig out the precious metal: gold.

Gravestones telling stories of life lost to the young, and the hardship under the scorching sun.

The ice-cold Odem of the murdered Japanese son and father at Kanowna bears the veil of mystery as to why and when.

Water was more valuable than gold, and only the trees are now retaining knowledge of the hardship of our forebears.

Touching a tree, walking over a graveyard, closing your eyes, feeling the wind –

Let's travel on a journey returning to the past.

Gum Leaves, Kalgoorlie

A Story Which Led to Christmas

Many Christmas day celebrations from my youth left some impression until today. We were living at the third floor in a four-storey house. At the end of 1940 to the beginning of 1960, where my Christmas story takes place, we were living in an apartment with one bedroom, living room, kitchen and amenities which were very basic. To have a bath we had to sit or stand in an old zinc bathtub; my stepmother filled it up with hot water or to make it more comfortable added some cold water. This was the privilege only at the weekend and during the week we had some quick cat washes in the kitchen water washbasin.

Morning breakfast consisted of a slice of bread which I held under the water pipe and sprinkled some sugar on it. It was a delicious sensation and very stimulating. Oats were also available and I mixed it sometimes with milk or water.

We were very fortunate to have had the Bakery at the ground floor and mother asked me, when we were short of bread, to go down the stairs and pick up the bread. This was the best exercise, fulfilling, because the bread was still warm. I could not stop my craving and had a bite from both sides of the bread which was very crusty but left me with a bad conscience and my mother was not very happy about it and I received my lecture, yet again.

Another time I had to pick up the zinc milk can and to pick up some spare milk from the shop opposite our house. It was a small shop with a counter and two round containers inlaid in the bench top. From there our milkman filled up my can of around one litre with milk.

This happened usually early in the morning and all the others competed with each other on how many times we could swing the milk can around without spilling a drop of milk.

Some were experienced, some were novice. Unfortunately this was not my day. When I swung my can around and reached the zenith of the swing, the can lifted off from the handle and the milk came spluttering down, and also missed my head by a few centimetres. The milkman must have seen it and I went in head down and asked if he would filled up again.

He must have had a good day and filled it up again with a stern warning not to be the champion of the milk competition again, which I followed with a pounding heart. I never mentioned it to my mother.

Both my step parents were working and I grew up with a key around my neck so I could go home any time.

I helped a lot at home, like washing up, cleaning the floor, pounding the rug and lots of other domestic things.

One day I cleaned the rug and when I put it back there was a small lump like a bubble left. I tried to smooth it over and hit it with my shoe to lay it flat.

Sometimes I also decorated the table in the kitchen where we all came together to have our meal.

Usually, this happened around twilight when our very tame budgie was in the cage. We put a white bed linen cloth over him so he could sleep well. Before my stepmother put the cloth over the cage she wondered that the cage was empty and questioned me about whether I have seen our little blue and white budgie.

I must have admitted that I hadn't, and we began searching for him and calling his name. I told mother that I cleaned the rug and there was a small dent in it. We lifted the rug and believe it or not there was our budgie. Dead! I got my lecture again.

Christmas was approaching and I wished I could get a bike from our friend at the North Pole.

Of course I believed in the man who could hear and see

everything. I told him I would never again behave badly and asked him, very politely, to fulfil my wish.

Christmas day approached. I had my bath, dressed in new clothes and was full of expectation. Still I had to wait before the door would open. We gathered around the table and had our Christmas dinner which was a rabbit – my stepfather brought it from the market. During the meal we had to spit out some small, round, odd-looking grey balls. Believe it or not there were still the pellets from the shotgun with which the rabbit was killed.

My parents disappeared and suddenly I was listening to ringing of the bell and the door opened to invite me into the room.

Firstly, I was overwhelmed by the light from the candle at the Christmas tree and the glare of golden glow of the ball.

At first I was not able to scan the full room but, as the fog slowly disappeared, there formed very slowly, before my eyes, the shape of a grey mass, which began to establish itself as a bike.

I was overwhelmed and tears were running down my cheeks. We then held our hands together and sang Silent Night.

The following day I had to learn to ride a bike and my first attempts were not very successful.

First off, my stepfather was holding the bike from behind and I pedalled along. He was holding the balance, I thought, but when I looked back, there was no holding and it was my first ride on my own.

Now, you remember, my parents were quite poor, so my dad had bought an old bike and he spent the month of December cleaning, fixing, and painting it. That present sticks in my mind more than any other, because of the amount of time my parents spent, along with the love that must have gone into it.

Many Christmas events went by, but to bring a close to my story, the last Christmas I remember clearly before I came to a 'fork in the road' and my life changed, happened when I was in my early teens.

My stepmother was in her forties when she became sick and had to undergo a consultation with the doctor. It became clear that her illness was serious and she had to undergo more tests at the hospital. She was diagnosed with cancer. Over a period of a year my stepmother went from a healthy weight to less than 40 or 50 kg. When Christmas approached she was allowed to come home from the hospital so we could care for her.

My stepmother was very weak, and there were days when I had to carry her in my arms from one place to another, and I also had to clean the pool of blood flowing from her legs. We decorated the Christmas tree as we never had before for this Christmas.

The custom of the time was for the meal to be had at 6pm and later the bell ringing from the door. I carried my mother in my arms to see the extraordinary light shining from the candle, thus wrapping her in the most beautiful atmosphere of the night.

We were singing Silent Night when my stepmother commented that we had opened the door for her to a better future.

After New Year 1961, she died peacefully at the age of 44 years.

After my stepmother died my life changed dramatically. I was seventeen years old.

A family is worth more than anything else in life.

The Leaf

And there was this one leaf
This fell onto the ground
And it was looking around
And there was nothing to see.
All the other leaves
With their lovely tree,
Were all huddled down.
So this one little green leaf
Fell onto the ground
He could no longer bear his life
He was the only leaf
His tears were wetting the ground.
Then the rain came down
And was full of acid
They planted some seeds
And the grass came up
And the cattle roamed around
And they ate the grass
And the rain fell down
And it was full of acid

Cheryl Workman-Davies

Cheryl has a passion for life and has always enjoyed the invisible world of words. Her observations and experiences of the world around her and her imagination are the inspiration for her writings. She hopes that you will enjoy the wide variety of pieces included in this book and stay tuned for more by joining her mailing list at cherylworkmandavies@outlook.com.

Underground

It's hot, humid, dark and noisy. 1.2km underground in a mine started 20 years previously. The ground groans as explosives blast hunks of rock into rubble. Rivers of gold keep workers employed in this less than glamorous vocation.

Ending Unclear

Lost
Found
Happy
Sad
Journey
Unknown
Unclear

A Furry Friend

A thin layer of frost tickles my paw
Wide open spaces give me joy
I run and run for miles on end
And when I tire I return to my two legged friend

Kalgoorlie-Boulder

Ochre red clay covers every plain
Up above the expansive Super Pit
Large trucks meld into small yellow blobs
Day in and out winter frost, summer storm, blazing sun
Sunrise fuchsia, magenta, canary, orange
'roos and emus wake and wander
The bush quiet and still

The Cloud

Fight it, fight it, don't let it win
Just when you feel OK something happens to make you remember you're drowning
Happiness is like amnesia
You forget that you're haunted by a darkness
A shadow that follows you wherever you go
But when the happiness dissipates
The friends go home
The laughter fades
Reality sets in
That shadow
That cloud
Hadn't ever gone away
It was here to stay
It was the constant
It was the norm
The thing that was always in the background
The fun
The wonder
The dreams
Hope
Vision
All were fleeting
But for a moment

All anomalies
The shadow was the thing to be counted upon
When everything was falling apart the constant was the cloudy greyness of life

Pigmy Possum

Ears disproportionate to body
Long pink curly tail
Sleepy black orb like eyes
Shelters from the rain

Geologist hunting for gold
Disturbs the sleeping soul
Cuddled inside a green RC bag
Rescued from impending doom

Safely relocated to a suitable place
Away from the dust, noise and commotion
In a few days all will be gone
But the memory of the possum will live on

The Printer

High pitched beeps. It's happened again. The machine demanding attention. Insisting that it be fixed. Paper jam the little screen suggests as the alarming beeping continues. Anxiously checking for that stuck bit of A4. Nothing. No paper. There's nothing wrong. Call the printer doctor. Because I'm done.

The Job Interview

Job interviews are painful enough when you're a stranger and the guy with your fate in his hands is an unknown. You'd think it'd be easier to interview with someone you know. Someone who has experienced your dedication and loyalty, endless hours of overtimes coupled with a cheerful disposition.

But what if the guy is a jerk and you're not the first to experience his road blocking ways.

You thought it was just circumstances back then, when he was your boss. You didn't have the courage or the confidence in yourself to stand against his will, to argue or fight for you.

The consequence of that inaction: now he thinks you're weak. It's partly because you're not in the particular club that he is in – you're not inside the circle. You're an outsider even when you come from inside. You're a woman in this man's world.

He holds this unconscious bias when he's ignoring your emails. Your interest in the position is laughable to him, he won't be wasting his time on you.

But you persist, you're not taking no for an answer. You're going to fight even if the outcome is predetermined by his attitude toward you. You email HR, the only time they come in handy is now, when you're going for this position that because of all the invisible walls and glass ceilings no one wants you to have.

Then this extraordinary thing happens: you receive an email from him. He wants to sit down and interview you.

How's tomorrow 2pm work? he says.

You reply, *Yes tomorrow is great.*

You ready yourself, preparing answers for all the typical interview questions; you know he won't take it easy. You assume HR will be there and take the time to cultivate and rehearse working examples of when you displayed teamwork, time management, initiative and an instance when you resolved a conflict. Things that they would know already but you're going to be prepared, they're not going to blindside you. This time you'll be standing up for and fighting for what you deserve.

It's 1.50pm and he's still not here. You're ready though, all the answers are plastered into your sub-conscious. You know what to say if only he would show up. The buzzing of the fluorescent light overhead makes you nervous and your fingers start tapping and your leg jigging. You try and shake it off – you need to be in the confident head space you were in two hours ago.

He appears at your door and niceties are exchanged.

"Shall we do it in here," he says, throwing you off slightly. You hadn't expected to be interviewed in your own office, but you go with the flow.

"Of course, yes, here is good."

"I only have five minutes because I have a meeting at 2," he adds as he takes a seat opposite you.

In your head you're disappointed at his total lack of sincerity but you shake it off.

He looks at you then shoots out the question, "So, what do you bring to the position?"

To read the rest, visit www.DustyStories.com

Time Faller

The sudden thump of body against ground tore me from my moment of self-pity and longing. Memories, like embers glowing red-hot and painful, burnt into my mind, would have to wait. She fell like a star from the heavens lurching forward unsteady, slamming into the vibrant red dirt on all fours. Her wild emerald eyes searched the landscape made up of eucalyptus trees, scrub and me.

She brandished a dagger in my direction as she yelled in a proper British accent, "Stay where you are!"

Quite an aggressive act for a teenage girl, but I didn't blame her. At that point in my life I looked like a vagabond with my tangled hair, matted beard, and skin coated in layers of orange dust, and I was only twenty.

"Whoa, please don't shoot."

She took a step backward, her eyes narrowed; clearly she didn't appreciate my sense of humour. I noticed her exposed flesh through her ripped up dress, the external expression of her internal disfigurement or at least what I expected from someone who was like me.

"It's OK. I'm Arthur, I'm a Time Faller too …" I reached out, my hand calloused from a lifetime endeavouring to make the most of my misfortune.

She considered my gesture and although the tension in her shoulders eased, she didn't take my hand so I shoved my hands into my pockets and continued on.

"I've been falling from 1801, England, so one thing you can be sure of is: you ain't there."

To read the rest, visit www.DustyStories.com

Leila Worth

I was born in England, my Australian mother and Yorkshire-man father later settling in Tasmania after the war. After my mother died, when I was 15, I lived with my aunts in Melbourne and studied to be an Early Childhood teacher. After that I travelled through England and Europe with friends, eventually returning to Australia.

My first teaching job was at Tennant Creek, where I met my husband, Ian, who was involved with mining. I followed him around the country, he working at various mining jobs while I taught at schools. We had three children – two girls and a boy.

We came to Kalgoorlie in the early 70's for the new mining boom.

I became involved with the local Penguin Group, and encouraged young children to take part in the Speak Up Awards, held by this group. I have always been interested in speaking and writing. I have been a member of the Goldfields writing group for about 3, maybe 4 years.

I am in my early eighties and still attending the writing meetings.

Song

Let's use some words to write a song;
It need not be so very long,
But with some rhythm, don't forget the rhyme,
We'll get the gist, though it may take a little time.
Words are special so much for them to do,
Ideas to give of what, when, why and who.
Use an adjective, a verb, a noun,
A setting, in the bush or town,
Or on a tall yacht on the sea,
Or desert island where 'home' doesn't need a key.
The world so wide where we can go,
Come join the fun – now don't be slow!!
Shall the story be of love, or loss?
Get a coin, give it a toss.
With some words, use as you please,
A Best Seller will emerge with ease.

An Important Room

This is not always actually in the house – sometimes known as the 'out house' in pioneering days for sanitary reasons – one may have to walk many yards through the back yard to spend necessary time in this important room. And hopefully it is private – a shonky door with a wire hook may be available.

The nicest 'out house' I've ever used was in an 'over the range' house in Queensland. The 'Privy' was well away from the house, with a double seat, a baby's one (Baby and I could be content together) plus an adult one. With the door left open one could see a bush road and have a lovely view of the valley. No cars or people. Truly a 'Room with a View'!

Then in Tasmania I was given the job of cutting newspaper squares and threading them on string to hang near the seat. Cheap toilet paper! And one always had something to read, an added bonus.

There was no need to flush – the long drop was enough! – a great saving of precious water.

Cleaning was non-existent really. A wooden lid hinged to cover the hole and usually just a dirt floor. Blow flies did often hang around, but somehow one managed. Part of the local wild-life!! Sometimes phenol was poured down the hole.

Younger/Older

The little girl walked positively into the living room. Dinner was finished an hour ago. She was in her pyjamas, with a penguin motif. Even on her head was a night cap designed as a penguin head.

"Hi," said her Dad. "All ready for bed, teeth cleaned?"

The little girl looked guilty. Grandma saved the day.

"Do penguins have teeth?" she questioned.

Great escape, the little girl skipped away.

To The Stallion

He stands so tall and proud, his head held high
His mane blows in the wind, his nostrils flare
Eyes scan the plain below, some mares go by
Loud neighs say 'Hi,' hot steam goes everywhere
He strikes the ground with one impatient hoof
Man sounds are blowing in the wind, beware!
He moves towards his mares – time here is now enough
He gallops, teeth gnashing, there is no time to spare
He leads the way, there's safety in the hills
The thunder of hooves is plainly heard
Leaping logs and rocks they flee with common wills
They've lost the men! A kookaburra's laugh that is a clever bird!
The stallion stops among the spreading trees
They're safe now with the birds and busy bees.

A Day at the Races

There was a bustling in the bush –
it was common knowledge in the town –
Twenty horses would be racing –
the prize – a thousand crown.
This was bigger than the Gold-rush –
from round the world men came –
Easy money is a draw and –
all tried it just the same.
They may not have found a nugget –
but now another chance –
A winner in the betting ring –
that would make them dance!

Still money in this Goldfields town –
though remote from maddening crowd –
Men found their suits and ties –
of fashions they were proud
Ladies too had gowns of silk,
and hats of Paris style
Now a good reason to dress up again –
they had waited a long while
With stoles and feathers and high heeled shoes –
crowds milled about below
The grandstand packed –
folk knew just where to go.

Jockeys too had on their silks –
owners' colours are essential
Mick is there with cap and whip,
looking reverential
In mounting yard horses parade
guided by their strappers
Not long now – 'they're off' cheered on
by the clappers
Gates fly open, then with a roar,
out to the track as one
Manoeuvres to the fence the aim –
that's the beginning of the fun!

Mick had the Irish Equine love –
he respected each fine horse
He had the art of 'whispering' –
a response would come, of course
Well forward in the saddle
he spoke in hushed tone
'Go now, my boy,' forward
they surged as one.
Only fifty yards to run,
now they were in front
The crowd, it roared –
on who did it punt!

Mick and Nugget didn't care –
they'd done their job with pride
Breathing hard they slowed,
but they'd enjoyed the ride
Escorted to the weigh-in yard,
Mick carefully dismounted –
Then 'all correct,'
Jockey's in and counted.
Back to the stable,
Nugget nudged Mick in the chest –
Mates for ever – they always are the best!!

A Piece of Furniture ... a Puzzle

There he sits, quiet and still. I guess he must be contented.

With four black feet on the floor, two horns protruding from his head, saddled and ready to go, waiting, facing the TV which isn't switched on at the moment, but no complaints from him!

But that wire trailing from his rear must annoy him a bit, though perfectly circular tummy is flat and neat, the 'stirrups' connected – ready for action.

His confident air exudes confidence in all he meets – letters and numbers flashing!

He doesn't demand to be taken for 'walkies.' He doesn't eat a lot and makes no mess – a perfect creature to live inside the house.

I haven't even bothered to give him a name. Oh well, maybe I had better mount, put my feet up in the stirrups, grab his horns, and go for a vigorous spin.

What a good mate he is!

(This creature is Leila's exercise bike.)

Panic

About 70 years ago I stood on the beach near Taree, NSW, to watch our three children play in the sea. The eldest was about six, the others five and four They had learned to love the water – Ian is a good swimmer. Soon they were paddling into water deep enough to swim. Splashing and chattering and laughing, they were unaware of a strong current moving them steadily down the coast and out to sea.

From the shore I watched helplessly – I am not a strong swimmer. Calling out was useless above the sound of the waves and water and the children were probably not strong enough to get back to shore by themselves.

How lucky I was, two young men with their surf boards saw our predicament and quickly volunteered a rescue! Soon three kids were safely ashore – no more swimming in that place!

That House in Tasmania

That house! It was old timber long greyed, gaps between some planks, one no longer horizontal after a slip in one corner. 'Guy Fawkes night' kids would love to use this for a bonfire. This house had small windows, most so dirty it would be hard to see in or out. Outside were the remains of a garden, an old rose bush near the very rickety looking veranda, a geranium trying to smile and look happy by putting out a pink flower among the cluster of buds forming the head. Now ancient but once loved and cared for by contented owners; Grandma in her rocking chair, sipping a cup of tea (the cup had a chip, but it was of fine bone china decorated with painted flowers)!

Mum and Dad met in England. We were stuck in Sale, Cheshire, 'til the war was over. Then Mum organised for us to travel to Australia – her sisters were in Melbourne. Tasmania was chosen for our new home as the climate change would be easier for Dad, a man from Yorkshire, to manage. He had had sunstroke coming out on the ship.

There was a lot to learn! The property selected was some land under Mt. Roland. The land there was already occupied by farms. Our piece had some paddocks and fences still managing to 'hang in'. Some hens were purchased, and a cow to provide milk and cream. In England Mum had made sure we had hens and eggs. Dad decided a horse was necessary to pull a plough and get the land ready for crops. A jinker was bought, too. Many a trip was made exploring along the old roads as Belle pulled us at a happy trot and no mishaps!

To turn the cream to butter a 'kangaroo' churn was acquired. When the handle was wound the bucket attached to the churn hopped up and down in fine style. Experience proved that too much enthusiasm and a gallop did not produce butter but a slow, steady beat and in two minutes – voila!! – butter-pats salted – perfect.

Surviving the ship voyage from England were cases and boxes and a tin trunk. Mum made sure she was well provided for a new married life with the family. I still use some tea towels and Irish linen table cloths purchased by Mum ready for the new life as homemaker – she still kept up her teaching.

Mum and Dad set such a good example of common sense; good materials and objects chosen with care and no wastage. It makes me feel so proud to have such sensible parents.

In the Garden

Sitting quietly in our garden is never boring.

I do not need human company, or a book, or a radio, using eyes and ears and the sense of smell to fully appreciate the joys of NATURE.

I purposely did not say "wonders" because these are always around – but have we really looked, and listened, and smelled, even tasted or felt.

I'm really lucky as Ian has enjoyed his garden all his life. He is often at Bunnings checking over the plant section, and is never loath to buy.

How much we deprive ourselves of because we haven't bothered to pause and absorb what is all around us: free entertainment.

I do admit that a cup of tea and a biscuit can enhance our sensory experiences – especially now as I pause to write and record. This will make our garden even more special.

Unfortunately, our front garden is not visible from the road. With a high teatree fence, passers-by can see very little. One needs to be invited in to really enjoy the garden, front and back.

Ian won the Best Garden prize. In fact three judges, all ladies, were hard-pressed to leave from the entrance under the double car port, they hesitated so long at the gate.

WWII England

All those wasted years as the war seemed to go on forever – black-out curtains, folk skulking around in the dark, bomb shelters, where crowds huddled in cement tombs underground. Constant hunger as Mums queued for food, with little choice – thank goodness for the Government opening up vacant land as allotments so folk could grow their own vegies. Family and friends in British countries overseas rallied to the cause – sent seeds, and Anzac Biscuits, and happy letters of good times still in the world.

Somehow there was loving and caring –Mum still taught Maths as a money earner, Dad built a pedal car out of bike wheels, chains and moulded ply wood so mum could take us kids to school and bring some shopping home.

Mum being a Melbourne girl with parents and sisters still safe in Australia booked the first available passage on a ship to get us away from the horrors of the war in Europe. After weeks of travel, we eventually reached Melbourne. Dad had suffered sun stroke on the ship. Mum sent him to get a job in Tasmania, and so we started a new life, with new challenges, but we still had time to have some fun.

Mum and Dad were always there for us, until Mum died, then my two sisters in Melbourne gave me a home till I became independent. I also chose teaching as a career.

I guess it was the foundation of trust and faith in each other that made a solid background for us kids, and to be responsible people ever since, as were our parents.

A Shirt I Never Wear

I bought that shirt a year ago – my wardrobe had the space.
It's hanging in my cupboard, not looking out of place.
I thought it would be useful – I could wear it all the time
The lacy weave looked cool – colour green of lime.

The problem is it doesn't go with shoes and scarves
that are my daily wear.
So there it stays, and me pretending not to care
So now it's really an antique – never seeing light of day
An Op-shop choice – so little money did I pay.

That shirt has survived a wash – the machine with agitation,
Then pegged up on the line – and got my adulation
The wind was very fierce that day – it blew and tossed the trees
My cold felt worse, and I was forced to sneeze.

More horrors still – the pegs let go –
The shirt disappeared then with all that blow
It hit the lawn and then the dirt and stone
My feelings too were hurt, the shirt's useful days are done.

But with love and skill I performed a resurrection –
As good as new, I gaze at my reflection –
My spirits buoyed, I'm ready for the day
Bother work – 'cos I'd rather play!

Now I'm heading out, and dressed up fit to kill
At the party my friends can look with envy (Oh go and take a pill!)
That shirt is surely better. I'm looking really grand
That shirt and I truly we're best in all the land.

It still lives on a hanger – but no longer pride of place –
Maybe I should pack it up and put it in a case.
Then memories will be all I'll have – but they will be enough
To make me smile, though life may be tough.

An Event in a Car

Jenny, with breakfast finished and dishes stacked by the sink, opened the front door and carefully locked it behind her, and moved down the path to the garage. Her pride and joy would be waiting, a secondhand Lancer, bought from a local car-dealer, and two sets of keys presented after she'd handed over her hard-earned money.

But there was no car in the garage!

She went back inside – the spare key should be waiting in the 'other things' in an 'Oddments' basket. No spare key!

Going back outside she was in time to see her little car coming in the front gate with Hugh at the wheel.

"Hi," he called. "I've just been to the local shop to pick up the milk and paper."

Jenny, too shocked to say anything, just looked, and went back inside. Hugh followed.

They sat at the kitchen table and had breakfast together.

Come Saturday morning Hugh said, "Why don't I put coffee in the thermos and we drive down by the river for morning tea."

They had a nice morning tea together.

A new week started – Jenny off to the local Bank where she worked, Hugh on his bike to the nearby High School where he was the Science teacher.

Out on the well maintained bush roads, Clem was busy, too, with his job driving a 'road- train', carting rocks and, hopefully, gold ore to the local mill. The road ahead looked clear. He relaxed and turned on the radio. Then out of the corner of his eye he saw a little red blot coming fast.

Clem slowed.

Next, the car, with Hugh inside, struck loose gravel, careered off the road and into the ditch and scrub beyond.

Hugh and car, a write off.

Dealing with HEAT!

Animals have the sense to seek shade, and water – both to drink and splash in or submerge their bodies in.

Sleepless and sweating in bed without even a sheet over me, I decided I needed a shower. With just the cold tap turned on, the water was still very warm with the hours of travelling 600 km overland in 'the pipe' from Mundaring Weir to Kalgoorlie. But it was good – wet body and hair, warm water for a minute, then bliss as the water evaporated. I drank a big mug of water, not from the fridge, just at room temperature.

These procedures were very soothing and satisfying. I relaxed. Maybe now I was ready to try to sleep in the bed!

We live in an old house with a big modern extension. Ian did get insulation put in the ceiling as a corrugated iron roof makes like an oven. Air-conditioning was installed too, but we seldom use it. With doors shut to keep out the heat of the day, shady trees and plants screening the windows, the slate floor in the main sitting room still feels cool to walk on – bare-foot is fine. Afternoon tea is seldom a pot of hot tea – water is fine!!

The "Long Kiss"

The "Long Kiss" is a photo that has a strong appeal to me.

The West Australian newspaper covered this in recognition of a photograph taken at the Perth Zoo in 1995 of a proud female giraffe and her calf at her feet, with his legs tucked under him, surveying his world, still new to him, head held high on his strong, long, baby giraffe neck, and mum reaching down nuzzling his head.

How important is a loving touch for a new baby; sight, too, as a baby zebra has an imprint of the mother's stripes, individual on each animal.

A baby can hear – a purr or squeal; taste – hot, cold, and sour; see things which may have as yet no meaning to them. But a loving caress is special, comforting and all is OK.

The William Grundt Memorial Library

I express my thanks and appreciation for the William Grundt Memorial Library with its broad, well-organised extent of literary matter – books, papers, magazines – and to the wonderful people who work there.

Now needing a walking stick to keep my balance, I was making my way to the Young Adult Section at the back, where our little Writer's Group has monthly meetings, with my bag of bits and pieces I use for the meeting, and a library book collected as I walked in. I was soon off balance and staggering and grasping for a non-existent hand rail. In a flash a staff member was by my side, passing me a small book trolley – on wheels and with handle bars – and I safely negotiated my way to the meeting.

Lal Nazzari, who organises the Writers Group, had organised speakers for the session – one, a Mr Morris from the Kalgoorlie Miner, who also volunteered help with our writing and providing exercises for our meeting sessions – including the 500 word challenge.

Then, when it was time to head home, I asked at the front desk for the use of the trolley to safely get to my car. That was agreed with no fuss. So I had a safe and wonderful afternoon with thanks to the many great Goldfields folk.

Kalgoorlie-Boulder is a wonderful place to live!

www.ingramcontent.com/pod-product-compliance
Lightning Source LLC
Chambersburg PA
CBHW070957180726
48291CB00004B/1329